February 5, 1993

Happy birthday Dan,
and happy travels.

Love

Sheila

LOCATIONS

LOCATIONS

Jan Morris

Oxford   New York

OXFORD UNIVERSITY PRESS

1992

Oxford University Press, Walton Street, Oxford OX2 6DP
Oxford New York Toronto
Delhi Bombay Calcutta Madras Karachi
Petaling Jaya Singapore Hong Kong Tokyo
Nairobi Dar es Salaam Cape Town
Melbourne Auckland
and associated companies in
Berlin Ibadan

Oxford is a trade mark of Oxford University Press

British Library Cataloguing in Publication Data
Data available

Library of Congress Cataloging in Publication Data
Morris, Jan. 1926—
Locations / Jan Morris.
p—cm.
1. Morris, Jan. 1926-   —Journeys.   2. Voyages and travels—1981–
I. Title
3465.M662   1992   910.4—dc20   92–6985
ISBN 0–19–212996–1

Typeset by Cambridge Composing (UK) Ltd.
Printed in Great Britain by
Butler & Tanner Ltd.
Frome, Somerset

CONTENTS

CONTENTS

INTRODUCTION

I t is a truism that the world grows smaller, and a truism especially obvious to anyone like me, who earns a living by perpetual wandering and writing. I have been doing it now for nearly forty years, and gradually the nature of the occupation has changed. Ideologies have risen and fallen, regimes have come and gone, airlines have amalgamated, magazines by the dozen have gone bust, I myself have grown, as the Americans prefer to say, older. More fundamentally, though, peoples everywhere have become more familiar with each other, and the idea of travel is beginning to acquire altogether new meanings.

I have had to adapt my craft accordingly. For one thing I seldom go to a city now, after so many years, that I have not written about before: I know the shape of the place, I have inner comparisons to make, I probably have friends there, and I no longer feel that I am a traveller there at all. For another thing, more and more I have been asked to write about places not for the entertainment of outsiders, but for the indigenes themselves: in this collection of eighteen essays, nine were commissioned by patrons in the countries they describe— so ready are people nowadays, and so interested, to discover how others view them.

For the most part, then, the pieces in *Locations* are not meant to tell readers how somewhere looks, or feels, or sounds, as most travel writings used to be, but simply present an individual response to a place—a wanderer's response, offering no advice, expecting no emulations, and (whatever the intentions of some of my patrons) certainly not hoping to contribute to the leisure industry. I gave the book its title partly because I liked the filmic sound of it, but partly because I thought it did not sound like the title of a travel book, but just of a book about places here and there, seen by somebody who happened to be around.

Justin Morgan and the Enjoyment Industry

*A*mong *the miscellaneous objects which lie around my library, few excite in me more various feelings than a small piece of iron piping which I have had framed and hung upon a wall. This essay about a journey through Vermont, written for the magazine* New England Monthly *and dealing with the impact of tourism upon one of America's most characterful States, will perhaps explain why.*

KNOWING that rooms were hard to come by, especially in what everyone calls the leaf-peeping season, the moment I entered Vermont I telephoned ahead to a motel. Three things I now know to be characteristic immediately occurred, one after the other.

First a very faint, scratchy, and peremptory announcement in an unknown tongue seemed to be instructing me to make the call again. I did.

Secondly an elderly lady's voice, announcing itself as that of Mrs Youdle, I think, said that, well, goodness, she never had rented rooms and wondered if she would be really fitted for it. Had there perhaps been some mistake? I tried again.

Thirdly the motelkeeper said she had no rooms. 'I wonder then,'

1

said I, 'where I can find one for tonight?' 'I wonder too,' said the motelier, and rang off.

This was not, I began to realize, going to be easy. When I was invited to drive along the length of Route 100, the road that meanders in an abstracted and picturesque fashion from one end of Vermont to the other, I thought I would treat the highway as a story, with a beginning and an end to it, and with luck a plot as well. But now, what with the baffling vagaries of the telephone system, Mrs Youdle's frail self-doubts, and the loveless absolutism of Mine Hostess at the motel, I saw that this was going to be a tale without a start, finish, or recognizable narrative.

I had better make it, I said to myself, an anthology.

Of course the first thing that strikes any foreigner driving along Route 100 must be the timeless, textbook continuity of everything. What age! What organic grace! What easy transitions, as the highway drifts in such a gentlemanly way between the hills, from one American age to another! The very beauty of the countryside, which better writers than I am have made fools of themselves extolling, is a concentration of everything we Europeans associate with the American origins: woods that sheltered Green Mountain Boys in the heroic days of old; fronded, reedy, log-floated lakes where barefoot children fished; pristine white chapels of Puritans; mountains where pioneers grazed their long-shanked pin-headed sheep; green flatland clearings beside clear streams, in which the hardy democrats of young America doubtless assembled with muskets, moose stew and deerskin hats to organize their destinies, working with their own hands, speaking their own minds.

The architecture, too, is a text of historical morality. In every window frame there resides an American truth, in every classical lintel an aspiration is embodied, and the whole white wooden marvel of it, strewn so profligate across the state, is one prodigious expression of the original American idea, ordered but free, decorous but cheerfully vernacular. I was moved and stirred at almost every corner as I wandered in fits and starts down my road, eating maple sugar all the way. The trees were on the turn, suffusing my progress in an almost unnatural glow of reds and golds. Wherever I went, Mrs Youdles were weeding their gardens, sticking notices on library boards, or presiding over chicken-pie dinners. In a daze I rattled over covered bridges, drank hot cider beside aromatic fires, consulted checkshirted ancients about the meanings of place-names, and generally submitted myself to the intoxicating spell of Old America.

And much of it was true. Vermont really is a glorious receptacle of the symptoms romantics like to identify as the American Innocence. I called one day upon the village school at Hancock, halfway down Route 100, and never did the ideal of an American childhood seem more comfortingly enacted. In a fine white building with a bell on top, the thirty children of the establishment were eating an ample Vermontian lunch at their desks—plump and rosy children in sturdy country clothes, almost every one of them born right there around Hancock, who looked up at me with freckled grins and stifled giggles almost like stage children playing parts in some jolly period play.

Another day I stopped off at the Adams family wood mill at Moscow, in Lamoille County, confidently expecting to find that the homely old plant beside the Little River would be into silicon chips by now. But no, the sample box of products in Curt Adams's office contained a wonderfully old-school variety of objects: napkin rings, toggles, things that looked like pegs or bobbins, things identified for me as honey dippers. And ah, what an idyll of old devotion is the John Woodruff Simpson Memorial Library at East Craftsbury, endowed by the granddaughter of a village storekeeper and housed in his own store! Meticulous as Victorian groceries stand the books along his very shelves, together with a ping-pong table for children of less literary leanings and a little collection of curiosities, assembled by the founder, that includes A Button-Hook Made by a Prisoner in the Philadelphia Penitentiary and an example of paper money that has been through the macerating machine at the National Bureau of Engraving and Printing. No charge is made at the library (which opens on Sundays, by the way, immediately after Sunday school). People can take away any books they like. All they have to do is bring them back. Do they always bring them back? I asked the librarian. 'No,' she replied.

Another essential of Old America is a sufficiency of feisty characters, and Vermont abounds in them—not in the gaunt, American Gothic kind, nor even the stereotyped Yankee, but in a subtler, craftier sort whose temperament reaches far back, I would guess, to the canny and self-reliant explorers of these northern woods.

Here, for example, is Rosanne Oates, sheep farmer of a certain age,

3

in Greensboro. She is coming up the steep hillside now with a bucket in her hand, gumboots on her feet, a woolly hat on her head, and round spectacles shining. Around her bounds a sheepdog, behind her a solitary pig in a pen looks wistfully after her, wanting to be tickled. Mrs Oates is a general's daughter and has travelled all over the place, but she lives truly like a settler in the woods. Her enchanting old house stands there as though the forest has just been chopped away around it, and her land tumbles precipitously away, beyond the pig, to the scrub and woodlands of the valley.

Huddled in a field to our left is a flock of her sheep, and when I mention a part-time farming acquaintance of mine living not far away, she says he is a customer of hers. 'In his farming capacity?' 'In his eating capacity,' she says, for she sells her lamb chops all over northern Vermont, and there seems almost nobody up here who does not know her by name. When I leave her to take the rutted dirt track for Hardwick and Route 100, she is already going back down the hill with another bucket of something or other, the dog at her heels, the pig getting quite excited down below.

Then at the Calvin Coolidge residence at Plymouth, where the president was sworn into office by his own father in the living-room, the lady who punches the tickets and supervises this archetypal shrine of the American Dream is Evelyn Whittemore. She has lived in the hamlet all her life, and is unstumpable. No question can defeat her, no request find her wanting. Your husband needs a mug to wash down his travel-sickness pill? Sure thing, no problem, let's see now, what have we got here . . . From beneath her desk Ms Whittemore produces an old shoe box stuffed full of miscellanea—'You'd be surprised, you really would, what people ask for, things for the kids and so on'—and sure enough, after sundry shakings and burrowings, she triumphantly produces a stack of plastic cups. 'There we are,' she says, 'isn't that just the thing now?'

Similarly, if you ask her about the late president, she effortlessly takes you back to his times as though they have never passed, as though Mr Coolidge has just written, as he always did when he was coming up from Washington, to arrange to go fishing with her dad. How lucky she is, I say, to live in a place where there's always a cup somewhere in the shoe box, where nothing seems to jar the progression of time, just as nothing disfigures the gold and brown of the mountains, the green of the mown grass, the clustering flowers around the open door before her ticket booth. 'Yes, I guess you can say that,' Evelyn Whittemore says. 'In that sort of way Vermont's a pretty nice kind of place.'

I snatched at a hundred such glimpses and encounters on my route, pungently illustrating, I thought, the unchanging Americanness of Vermont. I enjoyed the atavistic signs that ornamented my way, offering crawlers, worms, or buttercup squash. I laughed with the telephone operator who, miraculously obtaining a connection at last, involuntarily exclaimed, 'By golly, it's ringing!' I warmed to the storekeeper who, when I asked her if her village was as paradisaical as it looked, simply said 'Yep' and gave me a cookie. I wondered at the gravestone, near Searsburg, inscribed IN MEMORY OF 8 DEAD TREES and enigmatically explained to me as being 'just a big joke on Bob Pulaski'. I failed to notice the town of Glastenbury, recorded in the Rand McNally Commercial Reference Map and Guide to Vermont as having a population of three.

Best of all, I met Harold Childs, horsebreeder, of Harolyn Hill, near Tunbridge. On Mr Childs's land is buried the stallion Justin Morgan, the only progenitor of that superb American creature, the Morgan horse, not only one of the most exciting beasts that ever tossed a mane or pranced a set of proud and lively hoofs, but also the state animal of Vermont (the state bird, by the way, is the hermit thrush, and the state vegetable, it has lately been decided after a fierce contest with the fiddlehead fern, is the sweet corn). Justin Morgan died in 1821 and is commemorated by a stone on the public road near the Childs farm, but his actual grave is in a coppice well away from the highway, and Mr Childs kindly allowed me to go down there and visit it.

There is another, older memorial stone down there, and I mooched about it for a time, kicking the leaves around and wondering where exactly the bones of the splendid old horse lay. When I walked back to the farm I found Mr Childs waiting for me with a present. It was a short piece of old lead piping. 'Now this is true,' he said. 'Just here where we're standing now, there used to be the stable where Justin Morgan was kept, and when we was digging up there on the hill, we found this old lead piping, came straight down the hill here, used to take the water to the house itself—course that's not the old house, we pulled that down, built this one instead—and a branch of that pipe, it came right across the yard here and took the water to the stables. Now that's a fact.

'Now, I'm going to give you this bit of that pipe. You can say—and it's true—that Justin Morgan drank from the very water that came through this bit of pipe. You take it away with you, now.'

I took it gratefully, and I shall treasure it. 'I shall mount it on wood,' I said as I started the car to leave, 'and I'll have a plaque made saying "From this pipe drank Justin Morgan, the first of the Morgan horses."' Mr Childs tipped his hat politely, in the Old American way. 'Good idea,' he said.

But it gradually dawned upon me that, in spite of my glimpses of Old America, Vermont is actually not very American. It is true that the place-names along and around my route had the true all-American ring to them: Jamaica, Troy, West Berlin, Peru, Talcville (all the Johnson's Baby Powder you buy comes from the Vermont talc mines). Vermont is not really a bit all-American, though, and not quite traditional New England, either. It is like somewhere else altogether.

Several times I went into places of public assembly—a district court, a church, an auction room—and as I looked at the faces and figures around me, it seemed to me that they were hardly recognizable as Americans at all, but rather suggested, as James Bryce once said of New York, Europeans of no particular country. The grand racial mix of America, its blacks and browns, its high cheeks and its Spanish eyes, is notably lacking in Vermont. Nor do you often see the lean patrician kind so dear to celebrants of Yankeeness. In appearance, at least, your average Vermonter is a middling kind of person, middling tall, middling fat, middling handsome, middling plain—in short, rather unnoticeable, and very unlike the volatile metropolitans, the obese burghers, or the sun-kissed golden folk variously thought of by the world at large as being typical Americans.

I often felt myself to be in a separate country as I drove down Route 100, as though I were travelling through some wedgelike enclave jammed between Canada, New York, and the rest of New England. To the west the long line of Lake Champlain seemed to me like an ocean shore; to the east New Hampshire began to feel positively abroad. Nor was this merely fancy. Vermont's history has always been resolutely distinct from that of its neighbours. For a few years, from 1777 to 1791, it was actually an independent republic, and as late as the 1850s a resolution in the Georgia legislature proposed digging a ditch around the Green Mountain State and letting it float into the Atlantic.

6

Vermonters, it seems to me, are like ethnics in their own land. They are exceedingly conscious of their difference from other Americans, and they talk a great deal about outsiders, newcomers, and people from the south. And although they are lavish in their displays of stars, stripes, and American eagles, and have fought pre-eminently in all American wars, still their provincial pride amounts almost to nationalism. Theirs is the only landlocked state in the north-east (a fact evidently unappreciated by those Georgia legislators), and this makes them feel more tightly scrunched together than other New Englanders, more inbred, more severely confined within their own particular horizons—which are, as it happens, owing to the fact that nearly every Vermont mountain is covered with trees, invariably fuzzed and indistinct of outline, giving one the sometimes dispiriting impression that Vermont goes on forever.

In fact almost nothing that we foreigners think of as characteristically American can be found among these people. On the one hand they have little of the pith, salt, and repartee of New England myth; on the other, they are totally untouched by the cosmetic veneer of contemporary American convention—the instant sincerity, the compulsory smile. Vermonters are not only charmless of manner, on the whole; they are also, as far as I can judge, utterly without pretence, and give the salutary impression that they don't care ten cents whether you are amused, affronted, intrigued, or bored stiff by them. Hardly anybody asked me how I liked Vermont. Not a soul said 'Have a nice day!'

Also the more widely I wandered through the backcountry, east and west from Route 100, the more I came to feel that Vermonters were deficient in that fundamentally American urge, the spirit of competition. Appearances seem to mean nothing in this deplorably unambitious society. Vermont may be the land of the exquisite architrave and the delicate steeple, but it is also the land of the dilapidated barn, the undulating roofline, the cracked window, the collapsing fence, the loose step, the blistered clapboard, the lopsided cupola and the sagging porch. It may be elegant in the general, but it is gloriously unkempt in the particular. What kitsch mountains, what continents of junk would be created if one were to pile up all the jumbled objects that clutter the porches of Vermont, all the venerable sewing machines, broken basket chairs, daguerreotypes, bicycles, umbrellas, split sofas, bound copies of the *Rutland Herald*, stags' heads, disused freezers, and gilt-bound biographies of President

Coolidge that appeared to fill all the available space of every Vermont porch I ventured upon—not to mention the thousand and one antique shops that line Route 100 north to south, generally offering stock of such desperate banality that once, feeling I really ought to buy something, I was reduced to choosing the *Lamoille County Directory* for 1925.

Those millions around the globe whose notions of America are based upon soap operas would be amazed—horrified, perhaps—by Vermonters, who display no inkling of pride in material wealth or propriety. When the managing editor of a spanking little journal called the *Newport Daily Express* (with a circulation of five thousand, one of the smallest daily papers in the United States) crossed his legs, the better to emphasize an economic point to me, I noticed he had a large hole in the sole of his shoe. Mrs Oates's delectable farmhouse would have been repainted two or three times by now if it were in Texas or Colorado. Mr Coolidge, son of the state's most eminent native, lives very modestly at the back of the old family house, and the Vermont Museum, in the capital city of Montpelier, the central exhibition of Vermontiana, far from being any stately palace of territorial grandeur, is got up to look like a nineteenth-century hotel, and has a corner called Grandma's Closet where you are welcome to try on some properly tacky old Vermont clothes.

Of course this contrary variety of un-Americanness is partly geographic. Wherever you are on Route 100, you are a long, long way from the sources of American style, and in the north you are always close to the Frenchness of Canada. Road signs in French persist far down the road, and that Lamoille Valley directory of mine, explaining how some local names are spelled in different ways, offers as examples Greenwood, which is also spelled Boisvert, and Wood, which can just as well be Dubois.

There is nothing abrasive or domineering about the personality of this state. It seems very easy to adapt to, or to be absorbed by. All down Route 100 one sees signs of well-adjusted foreignness, a German ski lodge here, an English bookseller there, 'ethnic cuisines', as it says in the Central Vermont Vacation Guide, '[to] rival their cousins overseas'. Like most things in Vermont, the American melting pot seems to work here with a special calm and easiness. There is no aggression to it. Perhaps that is why so many eminent foreigners have chosen to settle here, sure that their identities will be respected. Alexander Solzhenitsyn, for example, behaves in many ways like a natural-born Vermonter, and seems to be accepted as nobody very untoward by his neighbours in Cavendish, a few miles east of Route 100. He shops with his wife at the village store, his children go to the local school, and if few people seem actually to have met him socially, well, that's nothing unusual in Vermont.

Besides, angrily writing away there in his house in the woods, Mr S. must feel reasonably at home anyway. It is not so very unlike Russia, after all, give or take a maple or a birch, white wooden farms or blue wooden dachas. I found my way one evening, just as darkness fell, along the winding country road that leads to his home, and found it in fact all too Russian, with the steel gate that guards the outer entrance to his property, the electric eyes that control it, the video camera above. The woods lay dark and dense around me, and dear God, when the dogs started barking far away among the trees, they might have been wolves barking out of the snowy steppes.

Speaking of Russia, the town of Moscow, where Mr Adams and his family make their honey dippers, was so named, it is improbably claimed, because an old saw used as a dinner gong by a local householder sounded to his neighbours like the cracked bell of the Kremlin. In 1933 the town was brought briefly to the attention of the nation when Franklin D. Roosevelt, eager in pursuit of his New Deal, plucked it from the national gazetteer as an example of rural self-sufficiency. Why, he said, in that little Vermont valley a modest sawmill, making knobs for the lids of teapots, had stopped the trend of migration out of the country into the cities. It was an example to all America. 'Every state', said the president, 'could be dotted with small country industries.'

Well, the Adams mill is still, as we know, making many a bob and bobble of Vermont timber, but alas, it did not end the move to the city after all, and the rural independence of Moscow has evaporated down the years. The school is closed now. The inn burnt down. The town's second mill, which specialized in wooden parcel handles, no longer functions, and Roosevelt's brave little Moscow is incorporated in the trendy ski resort of Stowe, a couple of miles up Route 100. The truth is that Vermont, which appears at first so permanent, so finished, is anything but changeless. Despite those serene appearances, life in this lovely state is distinctly variable.

One of the very few interesting things in the *Lamoille County Directory* of 1925 was an advertisement on the front cover that declared the Lamoille County Savings Bank & Trust Company of Hyde Park to be 'The Largest Bank in the World in a Country Village'. This was no mere hyperbole, I am assured; it was probably literally true, so prosperous was Lamoille County in those days. Today the bank is part of the Franklin Lamoille Bank, and its building on the main street of the little town still looks rich enough, but Hyde Park itself, like many another small Vermont community, recalls with nostalgia a more affluent past. From Newport in the north to Wilmington in the south, I heard repeatedly of industries closed, agriculture languishing, unemployment and disillusion.

The higher spirits of the children in that Hancock grade school are sustained all too often, their teachers told me, by Social Security. The unemployment rate at Newport, said my friend the editor, is among the highest in the United States. Mrs Oates says it is hard indeed for a Vermont sheep farmer to make ends meet, and Mr Childs no longer has Morgan horses up there on Harolyn Hill. The suicide rate is high in Vermont; there are many, many drunks.

Not much hardship shows along Route 100 itself, but if you take the side roads anywhere along its course you may detect all the classic signs of rural indigence: half-derelict shacks that would seem, were it not for their smoking chimneys, long abandoned; ramshackle trailers, stuck about with appendages of unpainted wood or iron sheeting; the scavenger feel of things, old car bodies rusting in grubby yards, mean dogs snarling and yapping at their leashes, scrawled illiterate signs— UTILITY TRAYLER 4 SALE, PUMKINS NOW—all the tokens of poverty and disenchantment, festering there in the heaven-sent glory of the fall.

These are symptoms of change, of the end of an era; but then change is nothing new in Vermont, and Vermont eras have repeatedly come to an end. Once this was an entirely agricultural state, living first on its sheep and its lumber, then on its milk and butter. Then other industries arrived, woodworking, quarrying, mining. Now, like any other such beautiful region in the Western world, Vermont is becoming more and more a place of recreation. It exists, very largely, to be looked at or skied down, as a location for second homes or for driving very slowly through, looking at the leaves. It is a prime showplace of the Leisure Revolution, the latest of the successive economic convulsions that have, over the generations, repeatedly changed the direction of capitalism.

A 1937 guide to Vermont singled out the village of Weston as another example of Vermont self-help in time of depression. Weston's gratifying search for a new and more vital life, it said, pointed the way for social and economic revival in all such Vermont villages. The book has proved prophetic. Every leaf peeper knows Weston now. It is one of the favourite sites on Route 100, with its Inn on the Green, its Mountain Stitchery, its Gourmet Brownie and its Feather Your Nest store. It has not one but two quaint old country stores, not to mention a Fudge Shop and a Cheese Emporium. It is a thriving plant of the enjoyment industry, as unmistakable, as inescapable, as the clacking looms, the whining saws, and the thumping steam-hammers of earlier profit systems.

All down Route 100, indeed, those homely proclamations for crawlers or pumkins are overwhelmed by the emblems of tourism, of which I offer you a few at random: An Occasional Place, A Special Place, Good'n'Yummy, Crust'n'Cauldron, Soup'n'Greens, 'Enjoy!' as an intransitive imperative, male antique dealers with hair rather too long for their age, female artists making ornaments out of painted gourds, snow spelled *sno*, shop spelled *shoppe*, over-enthusiastic use of the words *ambience*, *unique*, *truly*, and *experience*, as in 'the truly unique ambience of our dining experience'. This is the jargon of an immense and thrusting industry; these shoppes and sno-lodges are neo-mills, substitute factories. Ceres, the goddess of agriculture, tops the state capitol at Montpelier now, but if they were honest they would replace her with the figure of a ski instructor, a fudge maker, or an emblematic potter.

Why not? Although it is perfectly true that most of the beneficiaries of all this are, as Vermonters often tell you, out-of-staters, still it generates some local windfalls, I suppose, and as the aesthetics of tourism go, it is not too badly done. Sometimes, indeed, I find it hard to know what is old and what is new in this latest regeneration of the Vermont personality. The famously picturesque floating bridge at Brookfield, for instance, was rebuilt in 1978. The gloriously traditional cast-iron stoves made at Randolph and named Defiant, Vigilant, Resolute, and Intrepid, apparently after battleships, have been manufactured only since the 1970s and are named after racing yachts. 'How old is your house?' said I to a proud householder, surveying his evidently almost-immemorial wooden home, all primitive shingling and steep pitched roof at the top of a stubbly field. 'Six years old,' he said, 'but of course we weren't the first people in it.'

Consider yet another village, Warren, which lies on a short loop off

100. Here it is difficult indeed to distinguish the trendy from the traditional. There is an old village store, to be sure, but it has an annexe upstairs suspiciously called The More Store. There is a firehouse (Engine No. 1 a burly Maxim, Engine No. 2 a hefty Ford), but there is also a shop called Forgotten Furnishings. There is a covered bridge, but opposite stands a pottery with rustic implements artistically disposed upon its lawn. There is a Kids' Brook—'No Fishing over 13 Years of Age'—but there are also at least two antique shops. And what about the notice in the post office soliciting help in finding a Lost Critter, Sam the six-toed cat, who is 'too friendly for his own good'? Trend or trad? Native or newcomer? Rural or recreational? Danged if I know.

Here is change, and change more radical than your average American evolutionary process, the restless urge to alter things that lie near the root of Americanism. There is no denying that if in some ways it is fun, in other ways it is almost elegiac. Although there are people making fortunes out of changing Vermont, most of the natives I met, young or old, seem to think these effects mainly for the worse, whittling away at the old nature of the state, profiting a mostly alien few.

Perhaps it is only proper that autumn should be a festival in this state, when the tourists come from everywhere to admire the foliage in its dying splendour. There is much that is autumnal in Vermont. The visitors drive up and down Route 100 at funereal speeds, as though determined to prolong the evenings of their own days, and often I found myself drawn willy-nilly to the roadside graveyards of the place, where people with names like Abner, Joshua, Ebenezer, and Comfort lie in their ancient peace beneath dappled old stones and ungushing epitaphs. 'Where d'you live?' I asked one elderly citizen. 'Since my wife died,' he said, 'I've lived in the motel there,' and he pointed to a forlorn assemblage of huts around a car park behind us. 'And where are you staying?' 'Oh,' said I, 'the motel at the other end of town.' 'That's a nice place, too,' said the old man without conviction.

And the trees, which are the brazen heralds of the fall, strike me as elegiac in another sense. Not so long ago they covered only about a quarter of Vermont, the rest being cleared land, pastoral and arable land, creating a balance between the wild and the domestic that made Vermont seem like another Switzerland, so exquisite was the harmony, so gentle the green pastureland among the forests, so workmanlike the order of it all.

Today the proportion is exactly reversed, and three-quarters of this state is covered with woodland. There are too many bloody trees in Vermont! Often and again, settling down with my picnic upon some fresh meadow beside the road, it dawned upon me that the edges of the field were more raggedy and tattered than they should be, and I realized that the trees were slowly nibbling away at it, as they have nibbled away at settlements the length and breadth of the state, burying many a fine old farm beneath their undergrowth, and erasing forever the memory of many a stalwart clan.

Tourists love the trees. National forests, even wilderness areas, protect them. 'Six Miles of Natural Beauty', reads a sign near Granville, where Route 100 enters a particularly uncompromising patch of lumber, 'To Be Preserved Forever.' What an irony that the returning wilderness, cleared and kept at bay with such struggle by so many generations of pioneers, should be welcomed so effusively now, as it enfolds the Collectibles and the Forgotten Furnishings within its ambiguous embrace!

And now, how to conclude such an assembly of eclectics, as the tourist shoppes would say, gathered so randomly from such an indeterminate journey? Let me cheat, for my last Vermontian cameo, and leave Route 100 altogether, driving eastward almost to the New Hampshire border. It was there that another celebrated exile, Rudyard Kipling, spent some of the unhappiest but most productive years of his life in Naulakha, the house he built himself north of Brattleboro, and I thought before I left the state I would pay my respects to his shade.

The place is empty now, and fierce notices forbid trespassing on any account. I went to a house down the road to ask for advice, and failing to find any particular means of access, a common experience in Vermont homesteads, peered through a window to find myself almost nose to nose with a very Vermontian lady. Her face was framed, as in a Dutch painting, against a true vernacular interior—a suggestion of old dressers, comfortable spring-sagged sofas and bric-à-brac, and dimly in the background another more elderly woman, straight-backed as a school-marm in what I prefer to assume was a rocking chair. Four astute eyes looked out at me appraisingly. Well, what was their opinion? I asked. Could I take the risk and drive past those formidable signs to the house where the *Jungle Books* were written? They shrugged dispassionately, as Vermonters will. It was up to me, they said. There were said to be dogs up there, but so far as they knew there were no land mines on the way.

Vermont! Gingerly, gingerly, I drove up the bumpy drive toward the bleak old mansion.

| P | A | R | I | S |

Within the Périphérique

*I*n 1989 an English-language magazine in France, encouragingly but misleadingly named Paris Passion, invited me to spend a weekend in Paris and write an essay about it. They put me up in a small hotel near the Bastille, and all I did was potter around the city thinking, twice bumping into acquaintances, but otherwise alone. Preoccupied as I was then with the prospects of a federal Europe, with all that it might mean for my own country, Wales, I brought to the place all sorts of prejudices and ambivalences, not entirely untinged by envy.

PROUD Welsh patriot though I am, and therefore Francophile almost by historical definition (for did not the French come to our help in our last great rising against the English?), I generally get no nearer to the heart of Paris than the Périphérique. I shy away from the city centre like a horse frightened by a ghost, and the spectres that scare me are my own insular prejudices.

To name a few at random, I do not much like the songs of Edith Piaf, the boulevards of Baron Haussmann, the furniture of Louis XIV, the sound of Gertrude Stein, the vainglory of Napoleon or the conceit of Charles de Gaulle. I distrust, at one level, people who turn ideas into movements; at another, ideas themselves if too pressingly

15

articulated. In a paranoia common but not often acknowledged among Britons of my World War II generation, deep in my semi-conscious I probably resent the fact that, while London was blitzed in victory, Paris remained inviolate in defeat.

Yet I am haunted, as so many of us are, by the suspicion that Paris knows something other cities don't, that it has an advantage over them somehow, and is handling our brutal century more intelligently. So when invited to spend a long weekend in the place, I determined to restrain all bigotries, whether of taste or of bias, and look at Paris once more altogether from scratch—exploring my own intuitions about the place as I wandered footloose, Friday night to Tuesday morning, through what they used to call (but not lately, I notice, the idiom being too slushy perhaps for modern Paris) the City of Light.

I arrived after dark, and when I walked the next morning out of my hotel near the Bastille, almost the first thing I saw, through a bright-lit first-floor window, was a middle-aged scrawny man flexing his upper torso rhythmically before a mirror to a muffled beat of not very heavy rock. He clenched his modest muscles, he moved his head this way and that like a woman trying on a wedding hat. I could not resist stopping to stare, and doubtless sensing my gaze on the back of his neck, he turned and gave me, still twitching, a mordant, joyless smile. I thought of using him as an image in this essay, but when it actually came to the point I could think of nothing he was imaginal of.

Whenever I reached a high viewpoint I was at once excited and disturbed by the spectacle of La Défense, Paris's newest quarter, baleful beyond my Périphérique. Its skyscrapers seemed to me to stand there resentfully, brooding over their exclusion from the city centre. They have an allegorical look, especially seen through the imperial frame of the Arc de Triomphe, as though they represent a future being kept calculatingly at bay or in reserve.

Certainly with calculation, either way, for carefully selected envoys of Modernism have of course been allowed to enter the gates, and actually there is something about the ambience, or perhaps merely the design of Paris, that makes futurism seem easily at home. Place de la Concorde, especially after dark with its lights and streaming cars, seems to me very like a space launchpad, preparing to send its obelisk into orbit. The cruelly disciplined Seine, for my tastes the most overrated riverscape in the world, provides the perfect channel for those glass-roofed restaurant boats which glide beneath the bridges at night, headlights blazing, as slithery as vehicles from another planet.

Seen from the top of the Montparnasse Tower Paris looks an utterly modern city, laid out by computer beneath the vapour trails of its jets, while if you need a human figure to represent the coming age, you could hardly choose better than the solitary policewoman who, bathed in unearthly floodlight, patrols Place de l'Hôtel de Ville at midnight with her pistol at her hip.

The Centre Pompidou, which seemed a few years ago so reckless an imposition, already appears perfectly at home, its pipes and girders almost as organic as the sinuosities of Art Nouveau, its forecourt ever more reminiscent of the great square at Marrakesh. Like many an exaggerated emblem of Parisian assertion—the Arc de Triomphe, the Panthéon, the Eiffel Tower, the Opera, the Champs-Élysées itself— it has been reduced by sheer osmosis to a proper metaphysical size. As to I. M. Pei's Louvre Pyramid, I foresee that it will soon be cherished as an integral and indeed redemptive part of the monstrous palace around it. Already it provides, with its Napoleonic connotations, one of the city's most truly characteristic *coups d'œil*. Spouted around by its rumbling fountains, glassy as the sky above, seen through the gateway to the east it looks to me as though it has been dropped there ready-made from some meticulously navigated spacecraft.

In the Musée d'Orsay eight very, very small children sit on the floor around one of Gauguin's Tahiti paintings. They are addressed with an exquisite lack of condescension by their teacher, who explains in detail the composition of the picture, the flow of its colours, the relationship between its characters, human and animal. What fortunate infants, I think as I eavesdrop, to be born in such a city, to live among such beauties, to be treated with such courtesy! They listen with intense intelligence, their eyes shifting from teacher to painting and back again; but when they take up their drawing boards to copy the masterpiece, starting with an oblong frame to set the proportions, hastily I move on in case they one and all prove to be without talent.

I am agitated by the timelessly emblematic quality of Paris. It is not like other capitals, living for the moment and the cash. It is as though the whole place consciously stands for something or other, so that almost nothing is simply itself. Just as in Mao's China every single action, public or personal, had to fall into a political category, so in Paris I sometimes feel that every street, every event, every gesture is dedicated to some aspect of Parisness.

Elsewhere civic generalizations are generally out of date, overtaken by shifting styles and standards. Here they remain almost disconcertingly valid. The plan of the arrondissements still provides a sociological and aesthetic index to the city, and here as almost nowhere else the idea of a city quarter is not obsolete. There really are whores around Pigalle, there really are tramps beside the river, there really are Breton cafés around the Gare de Montparnasse, you really can buy a live common-or-garden hen on the Quai de la Mégisserie. Publishers visibly frequent Saint-Germain-des-Prés, and hardly had I read in my guidebook that the Café Floré, where I had stopped for a cup of chocolate, had lately become a homosexual rendezvous than I was greeted by an eminent gay novelist of my acquaintance.

Clichés come true, too. Parisian chic exists, Parisian live-and-let-live lives on—where but in this capital would the layabouts be left in peace on the warm floors of Beaubourg? Black people walk about Paris with such elegance, such panache of cape and flaunt of fur, that they might be living models of negritude. The Lebanese, the Vietnamese and the North Africans, however intrusive they may seem to the more racist of the indigenes, to an eye from across La Manche truly do appear to have been gracefully assimilated.

Just over the hill from Place du Tertre, which suggests to me nowadays a dry run for the forthcoming French Disneyland, I found myself wandering through a district which appeared so entirely and authentically petit bourgeois that girls still played hopscotch in its streets and neighbours actually talked to each other—I saw it!—out of their windows; and on the Sunday morning I walked from the Arènes de Lutece, where elderly gents were playing boules in the pale sunshine, to Place de la Contrescarpe, where the butcher and the baker faced each other in almost rural intimacy, where pigeons and drop-outs lazed bucolically around the square, and where I could hear from far down Rue Mouffetard the strains of an ebullient brass band.

How is it done? By a natural conservatism, perhaps a cautious view of change, and possibly not least of all by a serious acceptance of surprise as a constructive element of municipal style. The surprise indeed often seems as deliberate as everything else. The Metro is purposefully impregnated with variety, to dispel the sense of menace that other subways have; and when one morning I saw a small fire on the track down there, extinguished not with extinguishers (none of which could be made to work) but by a man jumping off the platform and stamping it out, I really thought it might have been specifically arranged for our distraction.

I helped a blind woman over a street-crossing near the Gare de Lyon. She looked particularly irritable, cross and demanding, but though born and bred in the 12th arrondissement, turned out to be diffidently gentle. It was a lesson to me not to misjudge the hard-mouthed, sharp-eyed, fast-shoving, middle-aged Parisian housewife, who may well be sweeter than she allows. I took the blind lady first to the post office, then to the pharmacy, and when I left her she said: 'Now I give you back your liberty.'

Sometimes it seems to me that Paris is marking time. Emerging from a recent past without, not to put too fine a point upon it, all that much honour, it is girding itself for a future to which it already seems much better attuned than most of its peers. Perhaps the Centre Pompidou digital clock, ticking away the seconds towards the end of the century, is counting down for the city itself; perhaps the escalators, elevators and walkways, which already move faster here than they do elsewhere in the world, are being imperceptibly speeded up, year by year, to accustom Parisians to the pace of the millennium. The ideas, it appears, are on hold—one hears of no successors to Existentialism or Structuralism—and French films, books and plays also seem to be holding their fire.

But then they are in the wrong language. That's the underlying reason, I dare say, why Paris gives me this watching, waiting, plotting impression. The most obvious anomaly of this city today, the most obvious cause for civic neurosis, is the fact that the French language has lost its cachet. Except among captive cultures like the Gabonese, I would guess that Spanish, German, Russian, even Chinese and Japanese, are all more in demand in the language classes of the world. Not to mention, of course, English. The Parisian complex about the English language must hit every stranger in the eye. Walking down the short arcade which connects the Centre Pompidou with the new Quartier de l'Horloge, I noted the following shop signs: Paris Basket,

Tie Break, New York New York, Scoop, Blue Way, Award's Academy, Yellow, Bubble-Gum, and Lady—all in 100 metres of Parisian shopping! The graffiti of Paris, if they are not of the mindless Manhattan sort which disfigure the Metro trains, frequently indulge themselves in Anglicisms such as Fuck Off Skinheads, Kill The Cops, or Crack Snack; as for Richard Branson's Virgin Megastore on the Champs-Élysées, it is like a people's temple, before whose alien gods all young Paris dances.

Nevertheless I still get the sensation that Paris may be stealing a march on us all. Cities do not think or conspire, of course, and one should not think of them anthropomorphically, but sometimes one senses that a profound historical instinct animates the spirit of a place, and I sense it about Paris now. I feel that it aspires to be, not the political capital, but the most resplendent and influential metropolis of the terrific new Europe that is soon to be born. Figuratively, those skyscrapers are held at a distance only while the future they represent is assessed and prepared for. The Centre Pompidou, the Pei Pyramid, the Montparnasse Tower have been allowed in as one might permit double agents into the halls of chancery, and the plan that won the competition for the new Seine bridge is, I note, the most insidiously Modernist of the entries. Technically Paris, in the 200th year of modern France, seems to me more ready than any other European capital for the opportunities of a twenty-first-century federal continent; only the language, only the magnificent language, preys on its mind, inhibits its manners, and breaks out in Franglais.

Wandering into Notre-Dame on a Sunday night, I found a choir and orchestra celestially performing Bach's Christmas Oratorio. The cathedral was full, a reverent multitude of young people sitting on the floor, if they could not get a seat in the nave, or simply milling about like me. It was magical. All Paris seemed to be there, singing its heart out or half-lost in the marvel of it all. When I discovered that the choir and orchestra came from West Germany, and realized that half the listeners were as foreign as I was, it only seemed more magical still.

So I left Paris as I came, in an ambiguous frame of mind. More clearly than ever I realized it to be one member of the supreme metropolitan trinity, with New York and London, one of the three cities where anything can happen, anything can be found, anything can be done, everyone comes. 'Drop a plumb-line into Paris,' Balzac said, 'and you would never find bottom.' It is an impertinence even to try to gauge the condition or the intention of such a prodigy.

Yet whether it be out of historicism or out of the collective unconscious of my own people, the city still leaves me uneasy. Just as I think I have exorcized my prejudices, new ones materialize. I feel that Paris, though patently more clever than most of its peers, is not necessarily more wise. I feel that given the chance, more readily than most capitals it would impose its will upon the rest of us. It seems to me somehow too harmonious for our times, without its natural element of chaos. I miss the unpremeditated clash of styles and patterns, and of all the street musicians who entertained me during my visit, the ones that beguiled me most were an unkempt English rock group—somehow they seemed more spontaneously outrageous than the rest.

For it is a humourless city at heart, I cannot help feeling; grand, of course, beautiful, brilliant, inexhaustible, indestructible, in many ways incomparable, but short on natural fun or fantasy. Perhaps that's why, when I drive by on the Périphérique, superstition keeps me out.

| O | A | X | A | C | A |

An Unquestionable Place

I have never been crazy about Mexico, and when I went down there in 1986 to write this piece for the Washington magazine National Geographic Traveler *all manner of things went wrong. There was an airline strike, my baggage was sent to the wrong place, my electronic typewriter failed me, and I was laid low by altitude sickness in Mexico City. Perhaps this helps to account for the hallucinatory pleasure which greeted me when at last I reached the main square of Oaxaca.*

DO you know those fairy-tales in which a wandering bucolic slips down a hole in the ground and finds himself in another world altogether, a world good, kind and shining? That's rather how I felt when, on my first afternoon in the Mexican town of Oaxaca, I walked down to the zocalo, the main square, for a drink before dinner.

It was like a benign hallucination, I thought. The great trees that shade the square, the ornate façade of the cathedral that overlooks it, the cafés that line its pavements—all were bathed in a refulgent light, casting the corners of the place into black contrasting shade, and making the movement of the people in and out of the darkness like the movement of stage characters in and out of the spotlight.

They were sufficiently theatrical characters, too. Nut-brown women cloaked in red, and dapper old gents with silvery moustaches, and gaggles of students like opera choruses, and small policemen with nightsticks, and rumble-tumble infants everywhere, and a blind guitar player doing the rounds of the coffee shops, guided by his urchin-familiar, and a gringo hippie or two, and barefoot families of peasants, stocky and urgent, loaded with shopping bundles and making, I assumed, for the mountains.

The faces were mostly dry and burnt. The movements seemed to me kind of airy, as though tending toward weightlessness. Among the trees some children were blowing up long sausage-balloons and letting them off with a squirt of air into the night sky, where they rotated dizzily away into the darkness like so many flying serpents.

Grandly, in the high white bandstand that occupies the middle of the zocalo, a brass band was preparing to perform. Instruments were gleaming, players' shirts were as white as snow. Now a clarinet, now a trombone blew a preparatory note or two, and the whole square seemed to be waiting for the music to begin. Sometimes there was a flutter of sheet music on a music stand, sometimes the conductor briefly appeared, and once I thought I heard the incipient oom-pah-pah of a waltz.

But no, though I hung around the plaza for two long drinks, and though the crowd still attended with infinite patience on white iron benches beneath the trees, I never did hear the band play in the zocalo that night, and this gave the whole scene, when I recalled it next morning, a tantalizing air of suspense, as in a dream whose denouement never quite arrives, leaving you to make up an ending of your own.

It was not a magic mushroom that gave me these agreeably alienated sensations in Oaxaca, but it might have been partly the altitude. Oaxaca, which lies some 300 miles south-east of Mexico City, is 5,000 feet above sea level. Its name, once you have learned how to pronounce it (more or less 'wa-HA-ka') sounds to me onomatopoeic in its queer combination of breathiness and romance; for the air of the place is necessarily rather thin, its location is lonely, and even in the light of day it retains an air of festive unreality.

It is unmistakably Mexico, but Mexico idealized perhaps, a Mexico almost without tears. For travellers of my own sensibility, often tempted to stay home rather than face the hassle of this endemically delayed, cancelled, closed-owing-to-national-holiday, mariachi-deaf-ened, taco-corpulent republic—for fainthearts like me, Oaxaca offers a salutary lesson. Even here nearly everything seems to go wrong, but when it does it all happens so gently, so elegantly, that you are instantly mollified. It is like a half-hour acclimatization session—half an hour in Oaxaca and you are indoctrinated into the frame of mind by which aficionados insulate themselves against Mexico's hazards, and live through them all with affectionate detachment.

In fact, Mexicanness is concentrated with especial flair in this small provincial capital. Inescapable are the specialized graffiti of Mexican protest, demanding better terms at the municipal pawnshop or new uniforms for museum attendants. Helmeted artillerymen stand guard over their barracks, and the police chief removes his gilded cap, but not his pistol, when he takes luncheon at Hotel El Presidente. In Oaxaca young people swap badinage in the best Latin Amerian style from high wrought-iron balconies across narrow streets, and there are memorials all over the place to the region's greatest son, Benito Juárez, bold leader of his country in the dangerous years of the 1860s, and to a plethora of local poets, musicians, teachers, and playwrights.

The first charm of Oaxaca is the charm of a Mexican provincial centre largely unaltered by the twentieth century, still proud of all its local worthies and contriving, to this day, to feel self-contained and respectable. It is like an exhibition town—a complete small city, built of green volcanic rock that acquires a golden overtone when the sun goes down. In a finely proportioned grid the streets of the old quarter are centred upon the zocalo, and if, like me, you find yourself perversely disorientated as you wander from Avenida Independencia to Calzada Niños Héroes de Chapultepec, that is certainly not the town's fault. Projecting their towers and domes above the rooftops everywhere, a whole family of seventeenth- and eighteenth-century colonial churches is standing there to guide you.

We are told that, there being little gold or silver in these parts, the Spaniards were not much interested in Oaxaca (though Cortes himself was so taken with the place that he made the Oaxaca valley the seat of his dominion). You would not know it from the monuments they have left behind—the intricate mellow constructions of pastel stone, the quaint multitudes of saints, beasts, and symbols, the cloisters fluttered among so serenely by black butterflies in the morning, echoing intermittently with such marvellously cracked and clashing peals of bells!

Faith sustained the Spaniards in this remote outpost of their empire, and manifestations of that faith still speak most tellingly of Oaxaca's colonial past. The Basílica de la Soledad contains a miracle-working Madonna, Our Lady of Solitude, and in its little museum a series of ex-voto pictures evokes with touching and sometimes grisly detail the marvels she has performed down through the generations. In one an eighteenth-century sea captain, alone upon the quarterdeck of his utterly dismasted vessel, observes with grateful astonishment Our Lady of Solitude coming to his rescue out of the heavens. Another portrays a Spanish gentleman who, 'having suffered from a violent apoplexy for six days without hope of life,' sits up in his nightcap and lace-sleeved nightshirt, abruptly cured. 'Keeping it in your memory,' said an old lady approvingly when she saw me copying these details into my notebook. 'Very good, very good . . .'

For Oaxaca is so small, and so amiable a city, that it is hard not to get involved. One evening in the zocalo I heard the tootling and stringing of a band, and out of a side street came a very cheerful procession. Four musicians led it—a trumpeter, a violinist, two guitarists, singing as they walked—and behind came a long trail of people holding vases of flowers and banners made of straw.

I joined this troupe at once, and around the square we paraded, trumpeting all the way. When we reached the doors of the cathedral a priest in vestments greeted us, and ladies with pots of flowers on their heads began a jiggly dance to the music. I enquired in what festivity I had been participating: the annual pilgrimage of the Union of Public Market Vendors, I was told, to the image of El Señor del Rayo beneath his golden sunbeams in the church.

Our Lady of Solitude is a proper patroness for Oaxaca, because the city really does stand on its own amid those bare-looking mountains of the south. Its appearance in the landscape is abrupt. Suddenly you reach it, suddenly you leave it. You are very soon through its urban sprawl and shanty-suburbs, and from the very centre of the city—from the bandstand in the zocalo itself—you can see the tawny countryside all around. Contemplating this fact one day, and looking around me in contrast at those sculpted cherubs and angels, those elegant façades and benignly guardian towers, I realized (not for the first time) the fantastic nature of these Spanish colonial towns. In no other modern empire was building done with such ebullient sophis-tication at such remote and improbable sites. The British built no Oaxaca in India, the French created nothing so exquisite in Indo-

China, and we must look back to the dominions of the ancients, to the overseas cities of the Greeks and Romans, to find a civilization re-creating itself with similar art and craftsmanship in foreign parts.

It is marvellous to conceive the passionate conviction with which, two or three hundred years ago, the priests and hidalgos of Old Spain must have set about reconstituting their society here in the southern Mexican mountains—the infinite care of design, the blinding certainty of ceremonial, the assurance of God-given privilege. In an antique shop one morning I came across the armorial bearings of some of the old Oaxacan colonial families—the Ramírez de Aguilars, the Bustamantes. How haughtily they had supervised the carving of their crests, I fancied, how meticulously they attended to the niceties of heraldry in that outpost of empire 5,000 miles from the Escorial! I asked a passerby if any Ramírez de Aguilars or Bustamantes were still around, and his response, though inexact, seemed convincing: 'Sin duda!—Unquestionably!'

Oaxaca is an unquestionable sort of place, as it had to be from the beginning, no doubt, in order simply to survive. Its stance is firm, but thanks to its streak of the merry or the celebratory, rather cocky. My trumpet-led procession around the square was nothing untoward, I gathered. It was a familiar expression of the town's personality, as comfortingly assertive now, when the shades of evening assemble from the highlands round about, as it was when the first Spanish Christians of Oaxaca fortified themselves with dogma and architecture against the unknown.

All this—the isolation of history, the isolation of geography—makes the character of Oaxaca feel all the more absolute. I love old, small cities in any country, and Oaxaca provides the authentic provincial stimulation. The reporters of the local paper, *Noticias*, are to be seen hard at work at elderly typewriters through their first-floor editorial windows. The undertaker reads a magazine among the gorgeously ornamental coffins of his premises. Going to the movies is still an event here, and people still make an evening of a lecture on art and theology at the Teatro Juan Rulfo.

In such cities, and especially in cities of Spanish origin, I always like to imagine that somewhere around there is an Eminent Local Historian who knows more about the town than anyone else ever will, and whose whole life is its history. Wherever I go I look out for this sage of my fancy, and in Oaxaca, sure enough, I spotted him, walking stately through his beloved streets in the cool of the evening. How unsurpassably distinguished he looked, how scholarly, and with what proprietorial knowledge he surveyed, as he passed by, each finial, grille, and sculpted angel.

. He was accompanied by the adoring wife essential to an eminent local historian, and when I saw them they were walking hand in hand up a flight of stone steps, surrounded on both sides by the blazing rugs and tapestries, the blouses and embroidered dresses, the sleeping babies and the leathery crones of an Indian crafts market.

For the Hispanicity of Oaxaca has been vividly, some might say violently, coloured by Indianness. This is the heart of the Indian south, one of the most Indian towns in Mexico, and a pure-blooded European seems to be a rare figure here. Even that historian is high of cheekbone, exotically deep of eye. On all sides you see the unusual walk, almost a falling on the toes, that is specific to the Indians, and you hear the arcane languages of the Mixtec, Zapotec, or Ixcatec— well, perhaps not Ixcatec, because according to the Oaxaca Regional Museum only nineteen people in the entire state now speak the Ixcatec tongue.

The Indians give to this venerable colonial capital an impression of intense and earnest diligence. They are always busy. They are always buying or selling, always on the go. In the covered market they move critical and unsmiling through the piles of mangoes, the pinioned hens, the scraggy ends of beef, the bags of dried grasshoppers or medicinal plants. At food stalls they eat their chicken in *mole* sauce thoughtfully, and all over town and the countryside they weave, embroider, carve, paint, or dream up grotesque masks.

Oaxaca is one of the chief centres of Mexican Indian craftsmanship, where the inherited skills of the indigenes show themselves on the very street corners, and every village of the Oaxaca valley has its own speciality of craft. At San Bartolo Coyotepec they make the famous black pottery of Oaxaca. At Teotitlan del Valle they make wool ponchos, rugs, and wall hangings. In several hamlets they make the comically painted wooden animals that now amuse people in craft shops all over the Western world, and in innumerable modest distilleries they brew Oaxaca's celebrated mezcal, a fiery liquor made from the leaves of the maguey plant.

The Indians seem endlessly productive—endlessly inventive, too, for every rug, every tapestry, every mask, every funny giraffe is different—and the life of the city appears to be governed by their calendar. If Saturday is Oaxaca's great day of the week, it is because the Indians come into market then from the villages all around. Those dancing ladies at the cathedral door, whose gyrations gave an antic delight to the feast day of El Señor del Rayo, were stalwart Indian women one and all. Juárez himself was a Zapotec. It is Indian devotion that gives fire to the Faith now, and the Indian presence animates the streets of Oaxaca with an earthy vivacity, and brightens them with primary colours.

European that I am, I have tried hard to imagine a European analogy for the combinations of Oaxaca. Architecturally, of course, it is like a Spanish hill town, with its baroque and rococo glories, its domed suggestions of Islam, its portentously *fin de siècle* Teatro Macedonio Alcala. But it is as though 100,000 country people from tribes long thought extinct were to be unleashed each day upon the municipality, bringing with them all the styles, attitudes, and traditions of an almost forgotten age.

They strike me as a people almost inconceivably old—a truly indigenous people, rooted in their own mores. In the regional museum, splendidly housed in a former convent, you can see how true to itself their style has remained down the centuries—the same suggestions of animist certainty, the same tastes for the gaudy, the decorative, the macabre, and the whimsical. One set of rooms in the museum, however, puts the Indians in a more formidable perspective. Here artefacts of an altogether eerier power look back at you out of their cases: jewellery of beaten gold, ceremonial headdresses, a turquoise-inlaid human skull, a rock crystal tumbler . . . These are the things found in Tomb 7 at Monte Alban, the majestic mountaintop capital of the ancient Zapotec, and they seem to brood there, beside the convent cloisters, like totems of a secret and by no means extinguished power.

And the source of that power looks down upon Oaxaca still from its mountain high above. The city called Monte Alban probably achieved the height of its glory in the seventh and eighth centuries AD, and was later converted to a royal necropolis by the Mixtec—those very same people whose languages we still hear, whose haunting faces we still see in the dappled light of the zocalo.

It is one of the supreme archaeological sites of the Americas, but it is surely more than that. It is also, as I see it, the colossal folk-memory of a race still alive and creative. A steep winding road leads you up there from the city, to the scrubland ridge that commands the converging valleys of the Oaxaca. There a vast grassy platform is surrounded by the arcane buildings of those pre-Columbian Indians: their temples, their palaces, their ball court, their supposed observatory. The wind blows brilliantly up there, out of the wide bare hills around, and there is mingled smell of dust and herbs from the shrubbery. The dry air carries voices with a strange clarity across the plateau; a dribble of tourist litter is scurried across the grass.

Far below Oaxaca lies, like an exquisite model among its foothills, and Monte Alban seems to look down upon it with a monitory air. Perhaps the presence of this peculiar stronghold casts some spell upon the town. On another evening I was up at Monte Alban when night began to fall. The lights came on in the streets below for all the world as though the old lords of the mountain had decreed it; and as I stood there so high above the little city, entranced once more, I swear to you I heard the band strike up.

An Owl in Paradise

I *am proud to say that after the publication of this essay in the* Independent, *London, some people in Norfolk Island pressed for the adoption of the Boobook Owl as the national emblem of the island. Whether or not they succeeded (there is a formidable rival in the Sacred Kingfisher, described to me darkly as 'a silent sort of kookaburra'), I shall always remember this delightful place as the island where the Boobook, like much else that is rudely threatened in our century, was saved in the nick of time.*

THE Norfolk Island Boobook Owl is saved! True, it will never be quite the same bird again. In its thoroughbred form it was reduced to one solitary female, stubbornly ranging the woodlands refusing to die out: it has been reprieved by the importation of two New Zealand Boobook males—not *quite* the real thing, but near enough, and sufficiently virile to have sired a couple of chicks already.

The Boobook ought to be the national creature of Norfolk Island, because the owl's struggle with destiny, fulfilled only by the cautious introduction of foreign stock, mirrors the efforts of the island itself to avoid extinction as a species. It is one of the few island paradises on earth which, while necessarily living by tourism, manages to remain overwhelmingly and unmistakably itself, and is thus an object lesson in the preservation of reality.

For it is social and historical reality that mass tourism most particularly threatens, and the reality of Norfolk Island is at once particularly profitable and particularly vulnerable. A green speckle in the South Pacific, about equidistant from Australia and New Zealand, 20 miles around and inhabited by some 2,000 people, the island is so startlingly beautiful that I would have called it the Corsica of the Pacific, were it not for the fact that its most obvious metaphysical characteristic is an almost preternatural respectability.

This is ironic, because its historical provenance is distinctly raffish. On the one hand its first settlements were British penal colonies of Auschwitzian horror, to which the most utterly recalcitrant of felons were sent from New South Wales to be bullied by the most despicably sadist of gaolers; on the other hand about half its present population is descended from the mutineers of HMS *Bounty* and the Tahitian women upon whom they fell with such lascivious abandon.

The penal colonies were abandoned in 1855, the mutineers' descendants, brought here from their overcrowded original homeland of Pitcairn, were long ago converted to fundamentalist Christianity, and Norfolk became what it still bravely tries to remain: an island Eden, redeemed from sin. As it happens there are no serpents on the island, and Eve's apple is figuratively replaced by a foliage of almost naïve charm, dominated by the Norfolk Island Pine, which is like a child's drawing of a conifer, and supplemented by a wonderfully innocent kind of subtropical shrubbery. There are rolling green downs on Norfolk Island, and sea-surged cliffs, and islets with Masked Boobies nesting on them, and little forests with Boobook Owls, we hope, quietly propagating in their glades.

Upon this idyllic natural order man has imposed a calm bucolic pattern. Geese, ducks, chickens, and horses meander here and there around the island. Cows have right of way on roads. Simple homesteads encouched in foliage are attended by comfortable vegetable gardens. Twice a month a ship anchors offshore with supplies, there being no harbour, and the island menfolk set to as a team or a family to unload its cargo in lighters through the surf—working with such unremitting comradely zeal that they might well be figures in some improving allegory.

*

It is like a ready-made theme park—scenic, folksy, educational, with stimulating elements of Grand Guignol, a natural Safari Park, a lovely bathing beach, facilities for Senior Citizens and safe fun for the kiddies. Any self-respecting developer would give his right arm for Norfolk Island, and the islanders themselves are by no means unaware of its potential. Postage stamps apart, their only export is the seed of the Kantia Palm: to sustain the pleasant standards of living to which the successors of the convicts and the descendants of the mutineers are now accustomed, Norfolk is obliged to sell itself, and besides those fortnightly freighters, several jet aircraft full of holiday-makers land each day at Norfolk Island's neat little airport above the sea.

These arrivals fit less easily into the Norfolk Island imagery, and they are greeted warmly enough, but with circumspection. The islanders' purpose is to make the most of tourism while keeping it in its proper place, and their island assembly has evolved a strategy of simultaneous offence and defence. On the one hand, it has declared, tourism is recognized as the basis of the island's economy; on the other hand the island is to be regarded as 'primarily the home of its residents, and not primarily as a tourist resort'. The bad effects of tourism, as well as the good, are officially recognized on Norfolk, and the island's three main tourist assets are exploited only with gingerly care.

The first asset is, of course, the almost fictional beauty of the place, and any ornithological protection society would be proud of the way this habitat has been preserved. There is no town on Norfolk Island, there are no high-rise buildings, there are no traffic signals, and there is only one street lamp. Even the buildings of the penal colony, with their horrific memories, have been decorously restored or allowed to crumble gently into ruin. The island feels like one delectable green estate, rolling, dappled, and surrounded by a cobalt sea in whose bays no speedboats howl, and on whose horizons by the nature of things hardly a ship appears.

The second asset is Norfolk Island's law-abiding homeliness, and here too the conservationists have done well. About half the inhabitants nowadays are incomers from Australia and New Zealand, but the manners and mores of the Bounty descendants—the Pitcairners, as they call themselves—remain paramount. Crime is so rare that nobody bothers to lock a front door. People habitually wave to passing strangers in cars, and call each other 'darling' with no irony or affectation. The old Anglo-Tahitian patois of the Pitcairners—

'Whutta-waye?', for instance, for 'how are you?'—is like a guarantee of kindness and probity, and makes the most timid visitor feel at home.

The third asset, an absolute tourist essential of course, is Shopping. Norfolk's import taxes are vestigial, so that an astonishing range of things arrives in those freighters from all over the world to be sold to the visitors at rock-bottom prices—from Moroccan caftans to Portmeirion pottery, from video cameras to musical boxes. Burnt Pine, the nearest the island has to a village, is one long street of cut-rate shops, around which, giving the place its single vestigial suggestion of glitz, predatorily meanders the island's declared optimum quota of 820 tourists at a time.

Only 820, maintained by controlling the number of hotel rooms and aircraft seats. But think what *could* have happened to Norfolk Island by now—not just the Theme Park, but the multi-storeyed resorts, the crooked casinos, the shady offshore companies, the dolphin pools, the money-laundering banks, the junk bond mansions! The key to the island's survival as a species is the fact that the small community of the Norfolk Islanders, though subject to Australian sovereignty, runs its own internal affairs, with an elected legislature under an elected president. Local values and aspirations are paramount, when it comes to planning permission or development policy, and all outside influences are kept under severe evangelical control. It is very hard to become an island resident, however rich you are; overseas ownership of tourist facilities, says the assembly's statement of tourist principles, 'is not encouraged'. About the worst (or best) one can find in the way of tourist sleaze is an English-style knees-up at a pub, or a kind of *son et lumière* in which people dressed up as convicts are dragged in shackles among the floodlit prison ruins.

All in all, although the threats of spoliation are always there, and although the Australians intermittently show signs of wanting to integrate Norfolk more tidily into the national structure, so far the little island, like that unconquerable Owl, has successfully stuck it out. Restricted imported strains have prevented sterility, and the place still stands recognizably in the line of Elysium—rare and excellent stock indeed, especially among islands.

L|O|N|D|O|N

Land of Lost Content

I *have tried to describe London more often than I care to remember, and never feel that I have got the city right—it is, I think, the most unfathomable of them all. This piece about a day in the capital, written for* The Times, London, *reads as though I have done with the place, but I dare say before long I shall be tempted to go back and have another try.*

I WAS sitting over my croissant and the morning paper in a coffee shop in Marylebone High Street when a tall elegant man in late middle age walked stiffly in and ordered a cup of coffee. He wore a long dark coat and a trilby hat tilted over his brow, and I rather think a pair of spectacles was inclined towards the end of his nose. He looked to me as though he had enjoyed perhaps rather too good a dinner the night before, and he emanated an air of unconcerned, if not actually oblivious, composure. I put him down for some mildly eccentric and very likely scholarly earl, of the Irish peerage perhaps, and thought to myself that only in London could one still see such a genial figure, at once so urbane and so well-used, more or less direct from the eighteenth century.

'Know who that was?' said the café proprietor, when the man had stalked perhaps a little shakily out again. 'That was Peter O'Toole.'

*

The thing about London is not that it is the most beautiful city in the world, or the nicest, or the most exciting, but that it is the most inexhaustibly interesting. It can set up endless trains of thought in the mind, many of them erroneous, together with fierce generalizations and prejudices. After a few years thinking about altogether less complicated cities like Hong Kong and Sydney, New South Wales, I was giving myself the pleasure of a day aimlessly pottering around the West End, and I thought the appearance of Mr O'Toole for his breakfast coffee a very proper start to it.

It was a lovely spring day, and at first all went wonderfully. London seemed delightfully serendipitous. I eavesdropped upon two young Indians in a supermarket, and discovered that one was telling the other the difference between English Heritage and the National Trust. I observed an old blue cardigan hung to dry, strung between a window-grille and an electric cable, outside one of the doors of the Foreign Office. I strolled all unsuspecting into the little cemetery called St George's Gardens, in Bloomsbury (weeping foliage over slab-topped tombs, just as in woodcut allegory), and discovered that somebody had placed a bouquet of daffodils in the sculpted arms of Euterpe, Muse of Music. I popped into a cavernous and apparently disused shop somewhere around Cambridge Circus and found it presided over by a gloriously Cockney auctioneer, selling objects that looked directly derived from the back of a truck with every comical flourish of the huckster's art. I looked in at Victoria Station, and thought to myself that no railway station is quite so station-like as an old-school London station—so vivid with newspaper-kiosks, so swarming this way and that with archetypal commuters, so emblazoned with announcements, so echoing and clanking and so haunted—by the smell of steam, by the ghosts of station-masters with top hats and watch-chains, by the wraiths of soldiers off to war and trippers on their way to the seaside long ago.

O, said I to myself, there's a lot to be said for London. What fun and freedom it still was, to be able to jay-walk across Piccadilly without some cop blowing a whistle and screeching at you! What an absolute declaration of Londonness the big red buses were, with their lumbering forms towering and jostling above the all but immobile traffic, and their platforms only waiting to be jumped on at traffic lights! No building in the world, for my money, represents its meaning more absolutely than the Palace of Westminster, magnificently self-important above its statuary, and there never was such an avian anarchy as the gobbling, bobbing, chattering, squawking, scavenging, strutting, pecking, variously haughty and ingratiating multitude of birds in St James's Park.

'I don't see the pelicans anywhere,' I remarked, apropos of this gallimaufry, to a passer-by whom I recognized as a Londoner by his unmistakably proprietorial air. 'Well now you mention it,' he said, 'I haven't noticed them around lately'—and something about the way he said it gave me a particular excitement. It was the feeling that he might have replied in just the same tone of voice any day since the Russian Ambassador presented Charles II with the park's first pelicans from Astrakhan. The most interesting thing of all about London, I thought at that moment in the sunshine, is its unequalled continuity— never entered by a foreign conqueror for nearly a millennium, and evolved without benefit of revolution.

It is not just the ever-apparent age of the place that gives me this particular sensation, but its mingled sense of knock-about change and conservation. Everywhere I noticed the symptoms. Here an ancient church suddenly looked brand new, here a frivolous new building utterly transformed some sombre prospect, here an office block tantalizingly looked almost as I remembered it, but not quite, having apparently been re-created in a kind of approximate pastiche. For a moment I thought with a thrill of horror that a new post-modernist tom-foolery really was going up opposite the Albert Hall, until I realized it was only the dear old Albert Memorial being restored to youth; and when I looked at Wordsworth's view from Westminster Bridge the whole metropolis, from the distant towers of the City to the Chelsea reaches, seemed in my fancy to be undergoing perpetual rejuvenating surgery, both cosmetic and organic, now a withered limb artificially replaced, now an eye-brow fashionably refashioned, transplants of one kind and another century after century, and hormone replacement as required.

Halfway through the day I saw a sign directing me to the War Cabinet Rooms, and down there in Churchill's bunker this sense of historical constancy reached a climax for me. Those ramshackle makeshift corridors—those cluttered offices and *ad hoc* defences—that oil-cloth map of the British Empire with a picture of HMS *Hood* in the margin—the convoy charts whose myriad pinholes represent a thousand actions, a hundred thousand lost lives—Churchill's chamber pot, the weather sign that habitually showed 'Windy' during air raids—the general sense of humorous dedication, loyalty and pride down there—all speak most powerfully of a people sure of itself, its style, its hierarchy, and its destiny. They play 'A Nightingale Sang in Berkeley Square' as one wanders around the place, and the bookstall attendant told me that people of a certain age often leave in tears.

After that, things began to go wrong with my day in the West End. Above the door of the War Cabinet rooms a plaque declares it to be an Award-Winning Tourist Site, and I must say this quickly dried any sentimental tears of my own. Increasingly I began to think, as my afternoon drew on, and I pursued my surgical metaphors, that the one procedure the city had evidently not endured was the insertion of a pacemaker. London's face had been lifted successfully enough, but its old heart seemed to flag. The badinage of that auctioneer turned out to be the only real Cockney I heard all day, and the longer I wandered, the further I seemed to stray from the spirit of Churchill's bunker, with its suggestions of amateur and comradely order—the rich man in his boiler-suit drinking brandy and talking to the president over the hot line to Washington, the poor man in his battledress ever-faithful with his rifle behind the sandbags at the door.

There were the usual gaping crowds around Buckingham Palace, the usual lines of coaches stretching away up Constitution Hill, but the royalist goings-on seemed to me curiously separate from everything else—no longer an organic part of the life of the city, but more like an Award-Winning Theme Park. What did he think of it all? I asked a street-cleaner, when I noticed him passing a mordaunt eye over the scene, and he expressed what seems to be the received popular wisdom about the monarchy at the moment. 'Well you wonder, don't you, if they're worth it? I was reading about where it cost'—but there, you know the sort of thing he had been reading about.

Still, at least the palace railings gleamed handsomely, and the Royal Parks around were stylish and free of litter. When I left the ceremonial heart of things, even within these privileged parts of the capital I found myself progressively more depressed by the slovenly, the slipshod, and the downright squalid. In the morning things had seemed spanking and sprightly. Now every other clock had either stopped, or still showed winter time, and in almost every public notice there seemed to be misspellings and ill-considered apostrophes. Finding a pair of fancy new telephone kiosks outside the

Hyde Park Hotel, I tried a credit card on the technology of the new Mercury system: the first telephone did not work at all, the second failed twice, and when I got through at the third try they didn't believe it was me, so totally unrecognizable was my voice.

Sometimes, like so many grumpy people up from the country, I began to wonder if I was really in London at all. Whole streets in the very heart of the West End seemed virtually emptied of English people. I even saw a Japanese riding a tricycle with a face mask over his nose, precisely as though he were in Tokyo, and half the electrical and computer shops seemed absolutely indistinguishable from similar stores in Manhattan; the same goods naturally, the same insidious feeling that in some way you are being conned, but most mysteriously the very same Indianified, Persiany, or indistinctly Arab young men who sell hair driers, floppy disks, and blood-pressure measurers in the permanently Closing-Down Sales of Fifth Avenue. When I walked past the Hyde Park cavalry barracks and found it guarded by a steel-helmeted and camouflage-suited trooper with an automatic rifle, it struck me that he might easily be protecting some strongpoint of an occupying army (no matter that he looked about 16 years old, and easy game, rifle or no rifle, for any self-respecting couple of toughs).

And somewhere in Oxford Street, towards the end of the afternoon, some kind of hallucination seemed to overcome me, and I found myself in a nightmare limbo. I passed a glittery casino, with doormen in fancy liveries—I glanced across at the bright and homely façade of the Dominion Theatre, where they were playing *42nd Street*—I pottered around the corner, and there was limbo. I was aghast. Who were these fearful people, of no particular race, of no particular kind, so crude and elvish of face, so shambling of gait, so shabby of clothes, so degraded and demeaned of bearing? Where were they shoving and sidling their way to? What language were they talking? What culture did they represent, what traditions inspired them, what loyalty did they cherish, what God did they worship?

They were just Londoners, of course. I seriously doubt if, visually at least, a less prepossessing citizenry can now be found anywhere on earth, than the citizenry which frequents those parts of Oxford Street. Everything about them looks uncertain and demoralized, from the allusions of their anorak slogans and hair-dos to the shifty slouch of their movements and the insolent way they throw their cigarette ends and wrapping papers around the streets.

By now the weather had deteriorated, too. The sky was grey, a fitful wind blew up, and I sat at a teashop to examine the bruising course of my emotions, since I thought how reassuringly London Peter O'Toole had looked that morning. I tried to convince myself that the great city was merely enduring a moment of transition—a moment of awkwardness, perhaps, that would presage the arrival of a truly classless, raceless, state-of-the-art society. I tried to believe that it was just the weather. I tried to find comfort in the idea that the *real* London, the *essential* London, was indestructible anyway. It was no good, though. I simply could no longer believe that this was the same capital, the same nation, with the same heart, that was represented by the War Cabinet's bunker.

I could not imagine this West End rising to some great communal enterprise with the old Cockney-and-patrician panache, and so I resigned myself to a conclusion I have long resisted, as a sign of nostalgic weakness and the ageing process: namely that the nation-State of England really ended with the Second World War. Its history was concluded then as absolutely as though a revolution had wiped it out, and its character can never be revived. Will it ever find a new style of its own, I wondered, this old-new, post-revolutionary, cosmopolitan European metropolis, released at last from a thousand years of tradition, and faced with the challenging freedom of a fresh start? And into my mind stole the insufferably patronizing text that the British themselves long ago inscribed upon the walls of New Delhi: 'Liberty does not descend to a people. It is a blessing that must be earned before it can be enjoyed.'

So I ran away, my tail between my legs rather, and took the tube to Euston. This was a mistake, for nothing could have given me a more dispiriting farewell. Not having been on the London Underground for a few years, I had no idea how miserably it had degenerated—the torn seats, the filthy floors, the mindless squiggled graffiti copied from New York, the dour and colourless people slumped there, the sweaty smells, the lurching of the elderly rattling rolling-stock, the occasional stop in deathly silence while the lights flickered, the sense of mingled resentment, fatalism, and endemic anxiety.

Just before I got out I happened to notice the Poem of the Week up there among the advertisements. It was a verse from *A Shropshire Lad*—the one about the land of lost content, the happy highways where I went and cannot come again . . .

| O | T | T | A | W | A |

City of the Great Hare

*I*n 1987 the oldest and most distinguished magazine in Canada, Saturday Night *of Toronto, celebrated its centenary, and its editors invited me to
write an essay about Ottawa for its commemorative
issue. I was proud to be asked, and perhaps a little
of my consequent hubris colours the the last para-
graphs of the piece.*

AT first, with its spiked and stippled towers above the ice-cold river,
Ottawa reminded me of Stockholm. Then on a windy Sunday afternoon I caught the savour of frying potatoes from a chip wagon in
Confederation Square, and was transported for a moment to Aberdeen. And finally I found myself thinking ever and again of Cetinje.

Cetinje? Cetinje was an obscure mountain village of Montenegro
until, in the nineteenth century, the princes of that country made it
their capital, supplied it with palace and opera house, stately mall and
proud memorial, and summoned to it the envoys of the Powers. In
no time at all it had legations on every other corner, while its rulers
married so successfully into better-known monarchies of Europe, and
implanted their personalities so ornately upon the little city, that in
the end Cetinje found itself immortalized in *The Prisoner of Zenda* as
the capital of that indestructible kingdom, Ruritania.

I am not suggesting, dear me no, that there is any element of comic
opera to Ottawa. No capital is more innocent of foolish pomp and

feathered panoply (though I must say there is a touch of the Ruritanian to the queerly green-uniformed officers, neither quite soldiers, nor altogether sailors, nor entirely airline stewards, who pour each day in and out of the Department of National Defence). But often enough the city seems to me, in its own self-deprecatory way, almost as exotic as Cetinje—almost as deeply in the middle of nowhere, almost as fiction-like in its nuances, just as resolutely equipped with the metropolitan trappings, as well-supplied with home-grown heroes, and embellished at least as adequately with halls of government and diplomacy.

Consider, before we go any further, a few improbable facts. In Ottawa mankind ate its first electrically cooked meal. In Ottawa one of the world's first multi-directional elevators takes visitors slightly askew up the parliamentary tower. In Ottawa I was offered one day, without a smile, pears poached in Earl Grey tea. Rideau Street ('Downtown Rideau! Downtown Dynamite!') has climate-controlled walkways.

Ottawa mints the coins of Papua New Guinea. Ottawa is inscribed all over with logos, acronyms, and cabbalistic initials, and dotted with buildings named for dead knights—the Sir Richard Scott Building, the Sir Guy Carleton Building, the Sir John Carling Building . . . An eminent prime minister of this capital maintained spiritualist contact with his departed terrier, Pat. The head of state to which Ottawa now owes allegiance lives several thousand miles away across an ocean, but its first presiding authority was the Great Hare of the Ottawa Indians, lop-eared creator of all things.

Isn't it a bit like Ruritania? I felt repeatedly in Ottawa that fantasy, or at least originality, was trying to break through, kept in check always by the Canadian genius for the prosaic; and I was gratified to discover not only that the distinguished Ottawa law firm of Honeywell and Wotherspoon actually lists a partner named E. Montenegrino, but that the Anglican cathedral in Sparks Street, believe it or not, was designed by King Arnoldi. Could anything be more Cetinje than that?

Certainly, for a start, no half-mythical Balkan metropolis was ever more baffling in its arrangements than Ottawa, capital of the most famously logical and sensible of modern states. If you stand exactly in the middle of the Alexandra Bridge, spanning the Ottawa River in the middle of this conurbation, you may experience a decidedly disorientating sensation—may well wonder indeed where in the world you are. Have a care, before you move an inch. Your left foot is certainly subject to the common law familiar to all English-speaking travellers, but in some respects your right foot is subject to strictures of the Napoleonic Code. If a policeman approaches you from the west, to charge you with improper loitering in a public place, he will probably charge you in French; if from the east, to make sure you are not planning acts of sabotage, probably in English.

Several separate legislatures are responsible for your right side, several others care for your left. Three different flags at least are flying all around you, and you stand simultaneously within the mandate, so far as I can make out, of the federal government, the provincial governments of Ontario and Quebec, the National Capital Commission, the regional municipalities of Ottawa-Carleton and Outaouais, the city administrations of Hull and Ottawa, and for all I know half a dozen other boards and commissions that I have never heard of.

Outside Canada I doubt if one educated person in ten thousand could place Ottawa with the remotest degree of accuracy upon a blank map. Most foreigners might just as well do what Queen Victoria is supposed to have done when she chose this singular spot for Canada's capital, namely shut her eyes and stabbed the atlas with a hatpin. Even here on the bridge, if you are anything like me, you may feel hardly the wiser. You seem to be in a kind of extraterritorial limbo, swirled all about by overlapping administrations, rival bureaucracies, ambivalences of geography, politics, the obscurer reaches of history.

Only the reassuring buildings of the Canadian confederacy, whose shape everybody knows from childhood stamp collections, make one moderately certain what city this is.

Actually even the Parliament Buildings have to fight hard to assert their identity on their ridge above the river. When I first came to Ottawa, in the 1950s, they seemed to be unassailable—a stupendous splodge of Victoriana supervising, like some arcane citadel, the homely logging town that lay around. Architecturally Ottawa then was absolutely *sui generis*, and one came across those astonishing buildings, far, far from any great city, as one might come across pyramids in a desert. They are astonishing still, and the federal centre of Ottawa in all its jagged majesty seems to me still one of the most satisfying of all architectural ensembles. It is, however, no longer sacrosanct in its uniqueness on its hill, but is invested on all sides, even from across the river, by siege-works of the ordinary.

This is partly just the penalty of national progress—we are in

Canada's century, after all. Progress has demeaned Ottawa with most contemporary building clichés, down to the latest curse of second-rate urbanism, mirror-glass walling. Almost every school of derivative design has had a go at Ottawa, from the Revolving Restaurant Movement to the Academy of Indistinguishable Hotels, spoiling all too many views of the wonderful parliamentary silhouette with insensitive height or flat-roofed background. Only the post modernists, whose skylines at least would be in sympathy with those prodigious old buildings above the river, have not yet arrived. But ironically the blunting of Ottawa has been partly caused by schemes of ennoblement—schemes to turn it into a worthy capital, and to unite its two chief parts, Hull on the Quebec side of the river, Ottawa on the Ontario, into a handsome and cohesive whole.

By its own lights this plan has admirably succeeded. This really does feel like one city now, with the Gatineau Hills as a lovely appendage to the west, and all the symptoms of a modern federal capital are here to see: wide grassy parks with tom-fool sculpture in them, pedestrian malls with globular street-lights, jogging lanes, historical markers, and a totem pole presented by the government of British Columbia. There is a purpose-made speakers' corner. There is a garden containing rocks from all the provinces, cartographically laid out. There is a dinky Ottawa Georgetown, New Edinburgh, where nannies and Volvos live. I don't think there are any Japanese cherry trees, but even they have their substitutes in serried rows of that ever-dutiful municipal flower, the tulip.

It is beautifully done, but there has been a price to pay. Just as the Montenegrins turned their heroic mountain village into a poor pastiche of Vienna or St Petersburg, so the Washingtoning of Ottawa has in some sense diminished the place. Year by year the relics of this town's rough-and-ready roots are disappearing. Raffish Hull, where Ottawa's bureaucrats have traditionally gone for liberating evenings out, has been half obliterated by massive office blocks meant to distribute the capital consequence more equably. Banished from the city centre are the great log jams that used to bring into this capital a romantic breath of the backwoods. The Thompson-Perkins Mill has been anomalously prettied up and turned into a restaurant, and the Carbide Wilson factory is genteelly preserved as a Heritage Ruin.

Even the railroads, those sinews of Canadian nationhood, have been cleared away. The terrific Union Station, a stone's throw from

Parliament, is now just another conference centre, fitted out, so my guidebook says, with a 'triodetic canopy of tinted acrylic'. The tracks have been replaced by scenic roads and walkways, the new depot is so far out that hardly anybody can be bothered to go there, and all that is left to remind us of the great trains whose steam whistles once reverberated across Parliament Hill is the faithful old Chateau Laurier, the only grand hotel in Ottawa where you can still open a bedroom window.

But all is not homogenized. Roughage still breaks in! Here and there you can catch a glimpse of what Ottawa was like before the developers and the National Capital Commission got going. Squeezed behind the functionalist ramparts of the Place du Centre, for instance, an irrepressible remnant of old Hull still roisters on. They are talking ominously as I write of curtailing its bar hours, but you can still drink into the small hours over there, as the voyageurs once did, you can still frequent, as Pierre Trudeau liked to, the dance-bars and bistros of the Promenade du Portage, the Lipstick Club still offers *spectacles pour dames* bang opposite the church of St Bernard de Clairveaux, and the tumbled balconied houses of the backstreets speak evocatively of yesterday's lumberyards and sawmills.

Better still, ever-palpable in Ottawa even now is the immensity of the landscape all around—one of the most monotonous landscapes on earth, but one of the most challenging too. Bears sometimes turn up in Ottawa suburbs, beavers impertinently demolish National Capital Commission trees, the air is pellucid, and from any vantage point you can still see the open country. Only half an hour away are the wooded tracks and lakes of the Gatineau Hills, where the log jams do still lie in the Gatineau River; on the very edge of town begin the farmlands of the Ottawa Valley, whose produce you can buy any morning in the Byward Market, just a couple of blocks from the prime minister's office. At least in my fancy the hush of the back country penetrates Ottawa even now: sometimes in the very centre of the city I seem to enter an abrupt inexplicable silence, broken not by the thrum of traffic but only by the swish of forest winds.

Best of all, here and there around the capital you may see, as a white fuzz in a distant prospect, as a deafening marvel on the edge of some landscaped park, the fierce white waters—those thrilling hazards of Canada which have haunted the national imagination always, which have meant so much in the history of this wanderers' country, and which remind the stranger still, even when tamed with sightseeing bridges, picnic sites, or explanatory plaques, that this is the capital of the Great Lone Land.

In some ways nothing is more dullening for Ottawa than being a capital. It has to reflect the mores, the aspirations, the styles of the country as a whole, and if there is one thing that is debilitating about Canada, it is the feeling that through no fault of its own this nation is neither one thing nor the other.

The British affiliations of Ottawa are fast fading, its citizens keep assuring me, naïvely supposing that I care twopence one way or the other. You would not know it in the church of St Bartholomew in New Edinburgh, a small and pretty Anglican church which has traditionally been the place of worship of Ottawa's governors-general. This seems to me almost as much a shrine of monarchy as a house of God. The governor-general has her own crested pew, there are flags and escutcheons everywhere, generals and noblemen are pictured all along the cloister, and there are signed portraits of royal persons, more normally to be found on the lids of grand pianos in ambassadorial residences, at the very portal of the sanctuary itself—as if to demonstrate once more that royalness really is next to godliness.

It is true nevertheless that one feels the old absurdities and sycophancies of Anglophilia far less here than in Toronto, say, let alone Victoria. Ottawa is above all a working town—once a lumber town, now a government town—and it has relatively few scions of old Canadian families perpetually rehearsing their bows and curtsies for the next royal visit. Socially it is not, I gather, particularly posh— among the 600 top Canadians listed in Debrett's *Illustrated Guide to the Canadian Establishment* I can find only sixty-three who live in Ottawa, and most of them are merely stationed here. Despite those knighted office blocks there is a strongly republican feeling to this capital: even the royal crests on official buildings, which strike me in Toronto as faintly insulting, do not dismay me in Ottawa, for they seem to be merely expressions of constitutional convenience, besides perceptibly contributing to the Montenegrin ambience.

But if the old spell from the east is waning, the magnetism of the south is inescapable. Directly opposite the front gates of Parliament, like an ever-watchful command post, stands the United States embassy, flag on the roof, iron posts in the pavement to discourage suicide drivers who might otherwise be tempted to come careering down the path from the Peace Tower, crashing through the Centennial Flame to explode themselves at the front door. The symbolism of the site is brutal, but not unjust, for there is scarcely a facet of this city, scarcely an attitude, an opinion, a restaurant menu, that is not recognizably affected by the presence of that vast neighbour to the south.

Ottawa first became nationally important as an *un*-American place. The Rideau Canal, around which the town coalesced, was built to give Canada a strategic route beyond the reach of predatory Americans. Today the US seems just down the road—if that. Nowhere in the world, of course, is now insulated against American culture: whether you are in Lima or in Peking, *Dynasty* will find you. In Ottawa, though, there is no escaping the fact that the United States is physically close at hand too, almost in sight, like a huge *deus ex machina* just over the horizon.

Working men in Ottawa have holiday homes in Florida—they call it simply 'down south'—and half the people I meet in this city seem to have just come from, or be at that moment about to leave for, Washington, DC. They suggest to me pilgrims, coming and going always from a shrine, and some of them indeed speak of the experience with a solemnity almost reverential. There are annexationists at large in this town, demanding the union of all North America, there are plenty of apologists for American actions, and in general Ottawa people appear less ready than Torontonians, say, to carp at everything south of the border.

Perhaps they have a more intimate acquaintance with the realities of power; or perhaps they keep always at the backs of their minds the image of that pleasant neo-classical building (architect Cass Gilbert Jr., 1931–2) foursquare and electronically protected at the gates of Parliament.

Not that Ottawans are at all American, still less British. They seem to me by and large quite particularly Canadian—in bearing, in manner, in response.

I went one evening to a public citizenship court, at which newcomers to the city, having completed the necessary preliminaries, were sworn in as Canadian citizens. The occasion provided a climax for a multicultural festival called Homelands '86, and took place in a cavernous echoing hall, like the most gigantic of all parish assembly rooms, beneath the stadium of the Civic Centre.

Was there ever an odder affirmation? At one end the great room was laid out with café tables, and among them Turkish children romped, Croatian musicians rehearsed national melodies, a Tibetan bistro offered brick tea with meat dumplings, and ladies in peasant aprons stood about munching hereditary sandwiches. At the other end, upon a stage, a solitary Mountie in full Rose Marie gear provided a lonely and slightly self-conscious element of pageantry, while an almost excessively benign lady dignitary, in gown and white tabs, welcomed the new Canadians to their fulfilment.

One by one those fortunates stepped to the rostrum, to swear allegiance to the monarch-over-the-ocean. The Croatians swung into another verse at the far end of the hall, and the Mountie shifted his weight, poor fellow, surreptitiously from one foot to the other. There were immigrants from fifteen countries, Poland to Hong Kong.

To me it seemed, like all processes of naturalization, somehow a little degrading, but to those actually undergoing the experience it was evidently an occasion of pure delight. There were smiles in every row, and enthusiastic applause came from mathematicians and house-wives alike. Eager children examined the documents their parents brought back from the rostrum, which looked to me suspiciously like income tax forms, and when everything was done, and all were, as the lady said, 'fully-fledged members of our Canadian family', and the Mountie had stood at the salute without a tremor throughout the national anthem—when all the formalities were over, the new citizens settled down with happy anticipation for the ultimate test of Canadian aptitude, a multi-ethnic folklore performance.

I laugh at it—I have an ironist's licence, not being Canadian myself—but I was touched really, and slipping hastily off before the first clash of Lebanese cymbals, from my heart wished all those hopeful people well. One of the true pleasures of Ottawa, actually, is its gentle cosmopolitanism. Not only is the place full of foreign diplomats both active and retired (for many of them, I am told, cannot drag themselves away from the scenes of their final *coups d'histoire*, or at least their last promotions), but nowadays it is also enriched by ordinary residents of many national origins. Iranians and Lebanese drive taxis, Haitians clean hotel rooms, Indians work in Japanese restaurants, and the most fashionable decorator in town is a Nor-wegian-Italian-Canadian, Giovanni Mowinckel.

Nearly all of them have been most subtly Ottawized even when they speak scarcely a word of French or English ('I recommend this one very hardly,' a waiter at Les Saisons said to me sweetly of the pineapple sorbet). Some acquired restraint, some special tact or mufflement, marks them out already as people of this city. If they know one English phrase at all it is likely to be 'No problem', or perhaps 'All right'.

What is more, Ottawa has gracefully mastered its own indigenous dichotomy. This really is a bicultural capital now. Government jobs are, they tell me, more or less fairly shared between French and English speakers; the population of the capital region properly represents the national proportions. In the most unlikely quarters you will hear French spoken in streets, or alternatively English, and in every part of the vast bureaucracy one language seems as acceptable as the other. I hardly heard a single sneer at bilingualism during my stay in Ottawa, and in my favourite restaurant of the region, L'Agaric at Old Chelsea, the waiter and I outdid each other in our determination to arrange for my cod's liver in each other's mother tongue.

I went to the closing night of the Ottawa Book Festival, in the National Library, and found it in many ways like the closing night of any other book festival. There were the usual literary groupies there, the usual lesser celebrities throwing kisses to one another, the usual culturally committed politicians and determinedly enlightened businessmen, the usual plethora of heavily bearded littérateurs (all of whom I wrongly supposed to be Robertson Davies, and one of whom very properly won the poetry prize). To my delight, it turned out to be a biliterary occasion. Two literatures were being honoured side by side. True-blue Anglo matrons launched into painstaking French before my eyes, gaunt and furious Quebecois relapsed without complaint into English. The winner of the non-fiction prize was one of God's own French Canadians, a handsome, merry, and amiable man who told me he had spent much of his life either in gaols or escaping from them, but who did not even bother to enquire if I spoke French—such a relief I always think when conversing with Francophone bank robbers of literary accomplishment.

Shortly before that event I developed a snivelling cold and, finding myself short of handkerchiefs, I took along to the National Library a face flannel instead. What fun it was to observe the good Canadians when, feeling the need to blow my nose, I produced this huge yellow square of absorbent fabric! One or two of them paused for a moment, but only a moment, in their conversation; some could not resist nudging a neighbour; most of them resolutely looked in the opposite direction, willing themselves not to notice. Blowing one's nose with a yellow face flannel is not, it seems, altogether the done thing in Ottawa.

Quite right too—it is not a pretty habit. Still, the reactions of those partygoers did entertainingly illustrate Ottawa's public personality. After a century of capital status, this is still on the face of things a decorous, tentative, discreet, conventional, sensitive and charming city. It is by no means lacking in fun, but is rather short of panache. Its humour is leisurely. It is very kind. It is incorrigibly modest— 'Ottawa! Why in the world would you want to write about Ottawa?'— and it bears itself with such careful dignity that even its flags seem to fly undemonstratively.

Of course there is limited room for flamboyance in a city so small. No more than 750,000 people live in the entire National Capital Region—only 300,000 in Ottawa proper. This is the archetypal government town, where almost everything is geared to the exertion of bureaucracy and the acquisition of power. It is obsessed with official matters, speaks habitually in officialese and subscribes whole-heartedly to official values. 'Why are you going to Paris?' a citizen of Ottawa is asked in a local anecdote. 'Why would anybody go to Paris? For the OECD meeting, of course!'

Like most company towns, Ottawa is compact and sociable. Within a few square miles everything happens, everyone lives. I had not been in Ottawa more than a few days before I had rubbed shoulders with the prime minister, the publisher of the *Canadian Encyclopedia*, the British high commissioner, the national librarian, the leader of the New Democratic Party and the editor of the *Citizen*. I sampled the buffet at the Parliamentary Restaurant. I had lunch at the house where Sir John A. Macdonald died. I took a stroll through the gardens of the governor-general's residence, and a man I met purely by chance on Parliament Hill turned out to be the federal MP for Ottawa Centre, who invited me to breakfast. The famous in this city are always evident: Margaret Trudeau Kemper can frequently be seen pushing her baby stroller through New Edinburgh, while anyone can walk up to the studio of Karsh of Ottawa, in the Chateau Laurier, and ask to have a picture taken.

Inevitably security is tighter than it used to be, but even now it is mounted in a familial, almost apologetic way. A woman in yellow taking pictures at a political demonstration readily identified herself to me as a member of the RCMP, collecting identity photographs for the files, and her male colleagues from the plain-clothes division, with their gunslinger stances and high CIA-type collars, might just as well have come wearing policemen's helmets. ('You guys are hiding everywhere today,' I overheard a uniformed officer tactfully remark to these less than indistinguishable operatives.)

The demonstration, as it happened, turned out to be a very Ottawan spectacle—there is a demonstration every ten minutes on Parliament Hill. This one was protesting against American policies, but with its posters, slogans, and flammable portraits of Ronald Reagan, to be burnt as the climax of the evening, it was not terribly savage, and was easily confined by the police to the opposite side of the street from the United States embassy. When four or five protesters peeled off from the others and tried a flank approach, I heard the following exchange:

POLICE INSPECTOR. Are you a part of this demonstration, which is forbidden as you know to go any closer to the American embassy?
PROTESTER. No sir, we are just Canadian citizens exercising our right of free movement.
INSPECTOR. Why are you carrying that placard, then?
PROTESTER. Oh, that's simply an expression of my own personal views, as a Canadian citizen.
INSPECTOR. I see. All right, go ahead then.
PROTESTER. Thank you, sir.
INSPECTOR. You're welcome.

So it goes in Ottawa—demonstrators given harmless leeway, policy politely defied, confrontation avoided, and free opinion maintained. The protesters went and chanted a few mantras outside the embassy door—*Ronald Reagan is no good, send him back to Hollywood*—and, having made their point, rather effectively, I thought, peaceably dispersed.

Can this be all, this common sense, this universal niceness? Surely not. That policeman and that protester probably knew each other from previous engagements, and loathed each other's guts. One must remember that this is the capital of compromise—or of equivocation if you prefer; Canada is permanent compromise, it seems to me. Province must be balanced against province, languages kept in kilter, immigrants smilingly welcomed, protesters warily tolerated. After a few days in Ottawa I began to think that perhaps some recondite

50

accommodation kept this city itself in balance—that some unwritten compact between the prosaic and the fantastic sustained its bland composure.

There are very few overtly crazy people in Ottawa, such as you see cracked by the pressure of more terrible capitals, but I suspect a hidden strain of suppressed eccentricity. They have not been ordinary men, after all, who have made this town. Some have been very odd indeed, and I have come to feel that if Ottawa were ever to relax its self-discipline and its conventions, a surprising gaiety, bravado, and individualism might bubble out, infused I dare say with neurosis. One thinks of Canadians as reserved by nature, but perhaps it is instinct, not temperament, that keeps all things in this country, great and small, so generally even and controlled.

I felt these intuitions strongly at the Laurier House, on Laurier Avenue, for two of the prime ministers who are commemorated there vividly suggest Ottawan opposites. Downstairs practical, predictable, pinstripe values dominate the replica of Lester Pearson's study, in which his personal memorabilia have been assembled. Everything here is orthodox. Here are those vapidly inscribed photographs of international celebrities essential to any statesman's décor, here are the scrolls, the keys, the plaques of esteem, the framed tributes, the robes of honorary degrees, and the coloured snapshot of the Lester B. Pearson Tulip. A quick sampling of the bookshelves shows me *The Edmonton Story*, *The Canadian Dollar, 1945–1962*, and two unsold copies of Mr Pearson's own *The Four Faces of Peace*. I leave feeling obscurely chastened, as though I have been found guilty of frivolity, and make my way apprehensively up the steep stairs to the living quarters of Mackenzie King, at the top of the house.

But another world is there—another two worlds, actually, for Mackenzie King was of course that prime ministerial spiritualist. At first sight his library seems ordinary enough, easy-going, comfortable, stocked with a couple of thousand agreeably varied books and furnished in a cozy bachelor style. But presently some unexpected features reveal themselves. Around the end of the sofa a dead but still remarkably carnivorous-looking cougar glares malevolently towards the door. On the piano stands the crystal ball through which the prime minister made his excursions into the occult. And in a corner of the room a single red rose in a tall vase stands before a portrait of the statesman's mother, with whom he was also in posthumous contact. The room is rather dark, and should really be dappled with the flickering light of a wood fire: but never mind, Mrs King's portrait itself seems to my eyes to be sort of phosphorescent, and her bowed white-haired figure casts its own fragile glow across the furniture.

Such a queer old cove on the top floor, such a steady head on the shoulders of the Nobel Prize winner down below! Their contrasting memories seem to reflect an Ottawan compromise. Pearson's memorial out there is his gravestone in the cemetery above Wakefield, a very boring block of polished stone. King's memorial, on the other hand, is his glorious estate of Kingsmere, with three fine houses on it, and acres of lawn, and splendid wild woodlands, and trails, and waterfalls, and a collection of miscellaneous ruins, from bits of a demolished Ottawa bank to a chunk of the bombed palace of Westminster, artistically disposed among the shrubberies.

I suppose it could be said, actually, that the most interesting thing about Canada is its alliance, whether fortuitous or contrived, between the fearfully dull and the colossally romantic. An entertaining piece in the magazine *Chatelaine* identified sixty reasons why Ottawa is so awesome. They included Canada Day in Ottawa, Louis'n'Frima's ice-cream shop, and the prime minister's wife, but actually I think the selection missed the most truly awesome feature of all: the historical and political mystique of this extraordinary little capital. For myself, I feel it most potently at the northern tip of Victoria Island, which lies in the Ottawa River just below the Supreme Court. I like to walk to the very end of the island, where the National Capital Commission's improvements peter out, and an unkempt patch of gravel and straggly grass looks much as it did, I imagine, when Ottawa was not here at all.

Down there, at inspirational moments, I have sometimes felt an immense and mysterious emanation of power around me, as seers feel energies in the presence of ancient stones. The river rushes urgently by, confused with swirls and eddies—white steam spouts from a power station—traffic streams across the city bridges—behind me is the foam of the rapids, above my head arches the tremendous Canadian sky—and on the bluff to my right stand the central, supreme, and emblematic buildings of one of the world's most titanic states. They look spectacular up there—such grandly convoluted structures, so gloriously towered and cooper-roofed, so exuberantly chimneyed, so elaborately topped with ironwork and flagstaff, so all-of-a-piece but so excitingly diverse, from the Nordic-looking Supreme

Court in the south to the great unfinished block of the National Gallery, and the lonely figure of Champlain the explorer on his high knoll above the river.

The force that I feel down there is not exactly political, nor even economic, but something more elemental—an emanation of sheer size and space, of huge rivers and distant mountain ranges, of oceans far away, of illimitable grain fields and awful forests and frozen bays and wild cold islands. Half a continent looks towards Ottawa for its leadership—millions of square miles are centred upon those very buildings on the hill above me—from Niagara to the north-west passage the mandate of this city runs. Now that *is* awesome! Talk about Ruritania!

Maundering in this frame of mind up the road from the island, I dropped in one morning upon the Supreme Court. The cases it was discussing were not very interesting, its judges (two men and a woman) said nothing pithy, the few spectators seemed torpid, the press seats were empty, the room was imposing without being exalting, and I was just about to leave when something astonishing happened. Suddenly the bench was bathed in an ethereal light, not unlike the luminosity of Mrs King, and simultaneously there appeared on TV screens ranged down the courtroom the figure of a portly attorney in Winnipeg, Manitoba, assuring Their Lordships, Her Ladyship too, that his client was without doubt, under subsection 22 of the relevant act, entitled to an appeal.

I was witnessing Lex Canadiana—electronic justice, projecting the images of guilt and innocence, truth and falsehood across sixty degrees of longitude to this grey building on the Ottawa bluffs. It was a process, I thought, of truly imperial splendour, and it turned the judges up there, who had until then struck me as a fairly provincial kind of magistracy, into an almost celestial tribune.

And this is the excitement of Parliament, too, just along Wellington Street—its vaultingly transcontinental, ocean-to-ocean range. Simply as a building Parliament is intensely moving. Its library must be one of the most beautiful neo-Gothic chambers anywhere, and its war memorial chapel brings the tears to my susceptible eyes—ah, those battles of long ago, those haunted names of foreign places and chiselled poems of grief—

> In Flanders fields the poppies blow
> Between the crosses, row on row . . .

53

But I was not, to be honest, much stirred by Question period in the House of Commons. It was a bit like the Supreme Court. Few blazing epithets were slung about, the wit was less rapier than rubber, and the MPs all seemed to be on their best behaviour.

In the course of the afternoon, though, a companion in the gallery identified for me, one by one, the antagonists below, and placed them for me in the vast geographical context of Canada. This changed everything. I was forbidden to use my binoculars—'Oh Jesus no,' said the guard frankly enough when I asked him—but even so I came to suppose that in the faces down there I could trace all the separate strains of the Canadian identity: pale faces of the wintry north, jaws from the Maritimes, Pacific brows, dark Quebec eyes, Indianified cheekbones, and that particular expression of expecting the best in everyone that I think of as peculiar to Ontario. I heard the varying accents of Canada, too, or thought I did anyway—here a flattened vowel, there a more than usually rotund diphthong, limpid cadence of the West, fervid flow of Montreal. Think of it, I told myself excitedly—the deputy prime minister comes from the Yukon, pretty well in Alaska, the finance minister comes from Newfoundland, more or less in Greenland, many of those parliamentarians down there have to travel for hours and hours before they can even catch an airplane to bring them here, and here we all are in a neo-Gothic palace.

But I was soon brought down to earth, or rather back to Ottawa, for now my cicerone drew to my notice a silent and serious figure sitting on a chair below the speaker. Having been crippled by strokes Mr Stanley Knowles, the senior parliamentarian in the House, has been given the privilege of sitting in that chair, in the heart of that immense political web, for the rest of his life. The sight of him was sobering, but strangely compelling too. He seemed to have been there always, an ageless oracle of Ottawa—last incarnation perhaps of that primeval Hare! He was earnestly following every word, and his head moved from side to side, as though to emphasize that whether the phrases were reaching him from farm or glacier, Atlantic cliff or Pacific creek, whether they were reckless or restrained, wise or foolish, from the left or from the right, in French or in English or in unknown dialect of the tundra, the one response they could be sure of in this city was mute attention.

So I swung here and there, between poles of ennui and surprise, throughout my stay in Ottawa. It was like being torn (in a considerate way, of course) between moods, and it may surprise the more abjectly diffident of Ottawans to hear that my visit ended most distinctly con brio. This is how it happened:

I am by vocation a wandering swank—I love to walk about the places I am describing as though I own them—and it cannot be said that Ottawa is a town for swanking. It is a town, as Thomas D'Arcy McGee once said, for 'industrious, contented, moral men'. Its Ruritanian aspects never get out of hand, its peculiarities do not generally show, and altogether it is too well-mannered a city for showing off, even to oneself. Besides, when I was there the weather was unusually balmy, making it feel rather less than its most dramatic self, and so even less conductive to delusions of superbia.

But on my very last day in Ottawa the *Citizen* warned us to expect the chilliest day ever experienced for that time of year, in all the recorded annals of the capital's climate. Instantly I sprang out of bed, put on three or four sweaters, and hastened down to the river past the canal locks. Wow, it was cold! I walked briskly along the water's edge, climbed the steps near Queen Victoria's statue, and found myself standing before the great central door of Parliament itself, surveying the awakening city before me.

The sun shone. The flag flew with an altogether unaccustomed flourish. The cold stung my cheeks and sharpened my spirits. And in the glory of the morning, there at the very apex of Canada, a mighty sense of swagger seized me. Down the wide steps I went in shameless pride, and the great tower rose behind me, and the eternal flame awaited me beside the gates, and all along Wellington Street the towers and turrets saluted as I passed. Nothing seemed ordinary now! Cetinje would have stood and cheered! As I paraded that bright icy morning through the streets of Ottawa, whistling all the way and blatantly wiping the drips off my nose with my yellow face flannel, it dawned upon me that if this went on too long, and if I were not extremely careful, I might start getting sentimental about the place.

But fortunately I had to catch a midday flight, so it never came to that.

|T|R|I|E|S|T|E|

Loitering on the Quay

*L*oitering in Trieste has been one of my favourite occupations for nearly forty years, and the place
has greatly influenced me both temperamentally and
artistically—when some years ago I wrote a novel
about an entirely imaginary city, time and again I
found that quite involuntarily I was employing
Triestine images and situations. I wrote this particular essay for Travel Holiday, New York, but it is
only the latest in a long series, and I hope it will not
be the last.

LOITERING, loitering along the waterfront—that's the essential, or
rather the symbolical activity of Trieste, the Adriatic port at the
extreme north-eastern corner of Italy. From my hotel window I can
see the city doing it any hour of the day, and half the night too. There
are people idly strolling. There are people just standing around.
Wherever I look there are anglers, unmistakably from the ranks of
the pensioned and the unemployed, fiddling with bait-boxes and
sometimes sauntering over to see how the next fellow's doing. In the
daytime the very buildings seem to stand in lethargic postures, after
dark even the lights look languid. The former Ocean Passenger
Terminal houses at the moment, so a large notice tells us, only an
exhibition of Rettili Vivi—Live Reptiles. The Seaplane Station has
not seen a seaplane for years. There seem to be no customers for the

launch offering trips around the bay, and its captain hangs around as lackadaisically as everyone else.

Once or twice I have seen a solitary poodle loitering along the quay. A few small boats loiter offshore, doing nothing in particular. Years ago, loitering myself down there, I sat on a bollard and started to write an essay on Nostalgia: but it never came to anything.

Of course behind those central quays there is plenty of life in Trieste, surging traffic, lots of shoppers, all the noise and movement of a big European city; and if we go downstairs and take the launch out into the harbour (the captain will be thrilled) we shall see that dilletantism is distinctly not what Trieste is intended for.

A century ago the view of this city from the sea, immortalized as it was in a multitude of prints and engravings, became almost a sub-genre of marine art. Sometimes the more elaborate pictures were dedicated in flowery script to illustrious persons, and they depicted a scene of unmistakable consequence. Ships dominated those pros-pects, some just tossing in the foreground for artistic effect, many more steaming or sailing in and out of the port like envoys of power and prosperity. Behind them Trieste lay most grandiloquently about its bay, and gave the impression that it too was By Appointment to greatness: and so it was, for this was the sea-gate of one of Europe's supreme political entities, the Habsburg Empire. Trieste was the port of Vienna, the open end of Austria—whose rulers were also Emperors of Hungary, Kings of Dalmatia, Bohemia, Transylvania, Croatia and Galicia, and Princely Counts of Tyrol.

Most of the ships have gone now, but seen from beyond the harbour mole the stance of the city remains the same. Trieste is all but surrounded by a harsh ridge of limestone karst, ineffectively softened by forests; against this austere background it still looks patently the gateway to somewhere or other, and bears itself signific-antly. A small white castle on a promontory looks like a lodge to its estate. Two lighthouses stand watch upon its approaches. A squat castle guards it from a hill. An enormous modern church stands like a blockhouse on the heights above. Around the port offices and palaces, hotels and banks stand in monumental parade, grey, four-square, encrusted with allegorical figures and vast mercantile emblems.

The eye of it all is the Piazza dell'Unità d'Italia (Piazza Unità for short), which is separated only by a wide boulevard from the central waterfront. For my taste this is one of the most satisfactory squares anywhere. Mostly shut off to traffic, paved all over, it is equipped with ceremonial flagstaffs, ornamental lamp standards, and a baroque fountain above which Fame displays the bulging prosperity of Trieste to the Four Continents. A sculpted king stands on top of a pillar, and wonderfully complacent nineteenth-century buildings stand all around. The Governor's Palace is tremendously gubernatorial. On the City Hall two bronze men stand poised to strike the hours with their hammers. The Caffé degli Specchi is warm, snug and gossipy within, a genial sprawl of tables outside. Best of all, the south-western corner of the piazza is occupied by the mightiest artefact of Triestino commerce, the old headquarters of the shipping company Lloyd Triestina, né Austrian Lloyd, resonant with success and crowned with clustered representations of Labour, Navigation, Neptune, and the like.

This piazza was once the point of embarkation for the entire Habsburg Empire—whose favourite acronym, AEIOU, stood for Austria Est Imperare Orbi Universo, or as one might say in English, Austria Is The Boss. It was then officially called (of course) Piazza Franz Josef. Here the imperial gentry, arriving on their sleeping cars from Vienna or Budapest, drank a farewell coffee or two before leaving by Austrian Lloyd for honeymoon, world tour, or diplomatic mission. They would easily recognize the piazza still—physically it has not much changed since their time; but they might be taken aback if, raising their parasols and resuming their kid gloves, they took a stroll around it before embarkation time (weaving an indulgent patrician way, we may see them now, among the small children who habitually play football between the flagstaffs, or wobble on tricycles around the Fountain of the Four Continents).

How disillusioned they would be! That Governor's Palace houses no imperial governor now, only an Italian regional prefect. The figures of the Four Continents have been sadly beaten-up by time, and Fame hovers uncertainly above a fountain that dribbles rather than cornucopially spouts. Almost nobody knows what king it is on top of the pillar. Petty bureaucrats, not shipping magnates, occupy the palace of Lloyd Triestino, the company headquarters having moved to more convenient premises elsewhere. And most disappointingly of all, to any visitors out of the imperial past, would be the blank that stands at the sea side of the square, the open side.

Once that space was spectacularly filled with the masts, sails, superstructures and belching funnels of an Empire's power: now, beyond the passing motor-traffic of the boulevard, there is usually only an empty patch of sky, beneath whose expanse the loiterers amble, fish, or write their indeterminate essays.

Trieste lost its occupation and its hinterland when, after the First World War, the Austro-Hungarian Empire collapsed and the city became an inessential appendage of Italy. It now occupies a narrow Italian enclave closely hemmed in by Yugoslavia. Hauntingly conditioned by this peculiar location, and by its own very particular past, for seventy years, on and off, Trieste has been in a condition of partially suspended animation. It is one of my favourite places in the whole world.

The imperial occupation's gone, but the imperial consequence is not all lost. In an attenuated way it permeates the air of the city, as well as the look of it. My hotel room looks directly across the former Passenger Terminal, where the Rettili Vivi are, and one night I was awoken by a portentous flashing of lights through my window. I rushed to the balcony, and saw that offshore a great ship was standing, brilliantly illuminated, while below me at the quay lights were blinking urgently on a police boat and a white ambulance. A few figures stood motionless and silent around, giving the scene an operatic impact.

For a moment everything was frozen, in the half-light of the waterfront, and I was reminded once more of those old Trieste pictures, in which empresses and archdukes sometimes come ashore, in picket boats from battleships, to be greeted by court chamberlains on the quay. I realized that in fact some unfortunate passenger on a passing cruise ship was being brought ashore for surgery, but still so evocative was the scene that long after midnight I lay awake fancying the major-domos knocking at my door to announce the arrival of Her Imperial Highness, or reciting in stately unison AEIOU . . .

Trieste can never escape its history, or its geography. To the west of the city the Latin world begins; to the east live the Slavs; to the north are the Germanic peoples. The old Empire made it a mixture and meeting-place of them all, an ethnic exchange, a civic mélange of languages and physiques and temperaments. Here you will find calm Italians, bourgeois Slavs, *Gemütlichkeit* with sting to it, and a thousand other anomalies and permutations of racial stereotype, bound into a unique whole by the pungent presence that is Trieste itself.

Big, solid, wide, heavily ornamented streets bring a touch of Vienna's Ringstrasse to this Mediterranean seaport. Big, solid, wide, well-dressed burghers speak of old money and traditional responsibilities. Trieste is not a picturesque place—handsome indeed, but never pretty—and is not in the least simpering. There are fine seaside promenades, but no sandy beaches; tourist attractions are mercifully few; the cars from Germany, France, Holland, or Sweden that stream through the city in the summer months seldom stop for long on their way to Greece or Yugoslavia. The city accordingly carries itself soberly, like a real working town, a town of professionals.

Trieste policemen wear dignified white helmets (and violent crime is rare). Trieste shopkeepers are very courteous. I went one night to the opera to see a revival of a work by a local composer, the almost universally forgotten Antonio Smareglia, and was struck by the thoughtful and measured responses of the audience—none of your cliquish hysteria here. I dined in several restaurants, and thought they were like so many clubs, so well-known did their clients seem at once to the management and to each other, so ready to discuss from table to table the latest local news in *Il Piccolo* (founded 1881). Indeed catching sight one evening of the chef bowing at me in a familial way from the innermost recesses of his kitchen, I felt quite like a visiting cousin myself.

After seven decades of Italian sovereignty, intellectually and artistically Trieste still offers echoes of old Austria. Its university is cosmopolitan, its opera house is a centre of social life, it is proud of its polyglot literary and cultural heroes—Italo Svevo, D'Annunzio, Stendhal, who was French Consul here, or James Joyce, who taught English at the Berlitz School of languages, started *Ulysses* in the city, and remembered it in the trenchant phrase 'trieste, ah trieste ate I my liver!' It is a great place for eclectic bookshops, demonstrations of meditational techniques, poetry readings, satirical plays, chamber music and exhibitions of multi-dimensional art. There is an art auction house on the waterfront, and sometimes if I peer through its windows during an evening auction the mellow glitter of the scene inside, the earnestly elegant assembly of dealers and collectors, almost makes me feel I have been transported to the Vienna of the Secessionists, when the professors, the art critics, and the connoisseurs met, pince-nez on noses, ivory-headed sticks in hands, opera hats on laps, to inspect the latest Klints and Schieles.

Nor are all the city's imperial functions gone—not quite. The liners no longer come to Trieste, but around the point from that languorous central waterfront, which is used now chiefly by yachts and a few fishing-boats, a more contemporary port is still fairly active. Tankers pump Gulf oil into the pipeline that supplies much of central Europe with its fuel. Colliers unload coal from South Africa, and at their own aromatic terminal container ships from Africa and South America deliver most of the coffee for the cups of half-a-dozen coffee-addicted nations. Ferries sail once a week (understandably empty, by the look of them) for Albania down the Adriatic coast, and a visit to the railway station still evocatively illustrates Trieste's traditional place on the map of central Europe. How stirring to know that to get to Warsaw you have only to change at Venice and Budapest! How comforting to learn that through carriages are still available to Moscow, Vienna and Belgrade!

It is the bus depot, however, that offers modern Trieste's most truly imperial experience. There the citizens of the old Balkan subject-nations—the Hungarians, the Romanians, the Bulgarians, the Serbs, the Croats, the Slovenes—arrive in their thousands to shop in this old entrepôt. They are like a despoiling army, fanning out predatorily across the city, except that they are shabby and diffident, are slung all about with carrier bags, and are in search not of jewellery, furs, or masterpieces, but cooking utensils, anoraks, shoes, suitcases, toys and household gimmicks.

For many years a Balkan market has catered especially for them, beneath the flowering chestnuts of the Piazza Liberta. It has a gypsy air to it, and its wares are modest but somehow picaresque: jeans of unlikely make, sandal styles of yesteryear, crockery that all looks like seconds, T-shirts with gnomic slogans such as Jumping Hi or Buldozer Landings. Through its crowded stalls the visiting Slavs wander stocky, colourless, and calculating, festooned with ill-wrapped packages and occasionally pausing, so the evidence shows, to write graffiti in the Cyrillic script. I was pleased one morning to see a substantial housewife from Bjelovar or Putnock inspecting a line of sports luggage designed, so its labels said, 'For Who Live Within Ones's Opinion For Our Own Adventure Instinct To Walk Around Metropolitan Jungle For Ever'. What could such a slogan mean? I asked her: but she replied with a very Slavic silence, perhaps because she spoke only Herzegovinan.

Towards evening the looting army returns to the depot to board its

61

buses for the journey home. So thoroughly has it pillaged the town by then that every cranny, locker and cupboard of its vehicles seems to be stuffed with acquisitions—packages dangle from the roof, boxes are stuck under seats, carrier bags are piled in the aisles; and while every housewife is inspecting her new stick-proof frying pan, and every child is playing with his electronically bleeping spaceman, many a thoughtful gent in double-breasted suit, one cannot help suspecting, is already calculating what profit his purchases are going to make on the resale market in Slobodskaya.

These forays out of the east are not half so furtive, all the same, as they used to be when the Iron Curtain was still clamped across Europe, and Trieste was like a rat-run through it. In those days the city used to feel unmistakably skull-dug, and I was vaguely conscious always of cloak-and-dagger undercurrents. Today it is still a place, I do not doubt, of many irregular traffickings, the passage of illegal immigrants, the illicit transport of gold and perhaps drugs from one half of Europe to the other, but the collapse of Communism has given its frontier commerce new legitimacy, and glimmers of new hope. Those multitudes of homely Slavs come to Trieste now, as they did in the days of the Habsburgs, as to a natural exchange and market-place.

I button-holed an elderly Hungarian, carefully writing a picture-postcard as he waited to board his bus one evening, and discovering that he spoke some French, asked him how he had enjoyed his trip to the city. He said it was an experience of nostalgia—by which he meant, I choose to think, if only in folk-memory as it were, that it had been like an outing in the old times, when the zithers played on the lurching wagons, the peasants danced in their embroidered aprons, and good old Franz Josef, the father of his people, still appeared on the postage stamps.

In European universities, I am told, a popular subject of debate these days is the nature of reality as expressed in literature—a controversy with artistic, philosophical and ideological nuances. The University of Trieste, in its bold modern block on the slopes above the city, ought to specialize in the matter, because in this city the lines between fact and fiction, as between past and present, or the explicit and the enigmatic, always seem to me especially uncertain.

The spectral remains of Trieste's old glories, the stately thoroughfares, the immensely rusticated palaces of finance, seem always to stand in a kind of limbo. Even the climate conspires, for it is an equivocal and tantalizing climate, its days sometimes grey-blue and stagnant, sometimes whipped into drama by the terrific Adriatic wind called the bora. The rim of the karst behind gives the place a shuttered, introspective feel, and the sea in front, so often empty nowadays, looks in the heavy days of summer strangely melancholy. Trieste is not at all a depressing place—on the contrary, I know of nowhere I would rather spend a few escapist days, but its perpetual air of expectancy, its constant hope that better times are coming, has long been muffled by resignation.

So the Slavs pour in and out, the traffic mills, the coffee is unloaded, the maestro raises his baton at the Teatro Verdi, the students continue their impassioned discussions about post-minimalism in the plastic arts, but still the city seems, generically speaking, to be loitering on its waterfront. When the sensations of Trieste feel particularly opaque I sometimes find myself wondering if it really exists at all. Have I imagined it? Was the Rettili Vivi exhibition only a dream? Was there ever really such a composer as Antonio Smareglia? Are the scavenging Herzegovinans purely imaginary? Even now I am not sure if I actually did see a particular couple of loiterers I think I observed on the front one Saturday evening. One was a young man, nattily dressed in suit and brown hat, tootling on a shepherd's flute. His companion was older, and was attached by complex apparatus to a variety of instruments—bagpipes, drums, cymbals, a triangle I think—and in order to beat the big drum he had to move in an abrupt but creaky shuffle. Slowly and sporadically these engaging fellows pottered down the waterfront, tootling and drumming and shuffling.

They did not strike me as being in the least eccentric, as I watched them from my balcony. Trieste is not an oddball city. On the contrary, they had rather an Establishment air, and it crossed my mind that they might be there to greet the empress, when she disembarked from her battleship later that night.

| W | E | S | T | P | O | I | N | T |

'Beat Louisville Sir'

I found myself so depressed by the state of America in 1991 that I picked up a car in Manhattan and drove up the Hudson River, intending to wander for a few days in search of consolation. In the event I got no further than West Point, and this essay for Travel Holiday, New York, *explains why.*

AFTER dark one evening I went down alone to the Plain, the great playing-field and parade ground of the US Military Academy at West Point. This was like an American fiction. A moon was rising, the Hudson lay dark and velvety below, and across the grass a solitary skunk came snuffling through the dusk. Now and then aircraft winked their way overhead. A train wailed somewhere. A tug and its barges laboured upstream towards Albany. A military police car coasted curiously by. There was not another soul about, down there above the river, but in the great monastic buildings of the Academy, dimly crowned by their chapel tower, a myriad lights steadily and silently burnt.

Four thousand four hundred young American men and women, I knew, were hard at work in there: steadfast before computer screens, deep into ballistic theories, economic principles, translations from the Russian, comparative equations or historical relevances. They were being prepared as an élite, an officer corps to lead the armies of the Republic into a world subject more than ever to American power and decision—the world of the Pax Americana. My few minutes alone

64

there seemed to me an almost transcendental experience: one of those moments of travel when history, place and circumstance all seem in collusion to proclaim some truth or other, if we can only discover what it is.

The police car came back again. 'You okay, ma'am?' Sure, I said, quite okay: just watching the skunk.

It was true that I had never seen a skunk in the wild before, but in fact I was contemplating the moment. I cannot deny that I was greatly depressed just then by the condition of the United States, which seemed more than usually sunk in crime, corruption and hypocrisy, bewildered by racialism and enervated by crackpot introspections. West Point was like a world of its own, a place where the old American values counted still, honour and duty were watchwords and to tell a lie was to betray one's heritage: a place too, so it appeared that evening, where purpose was so exactly matched by appearance that the whole scene became an allegory.

Next day I went back in daylight, and saw the future élite for myself—classes of '92 to '95. Every day at noon the entire Corps of Cadets parades in its grey working uniform between the statues of Eisenhower and MacArthur, with Washington on his high plinth in the middle. Some of the West Point mystique, accumulated since the academy's foundation in 1802, is then on display for any passer-by to see. Ensigns flutter. A band plays. Swords flash. Tradition's Long Grey Line is regimentally massed. And one of the place's better-known peculiarities is publicly demonstrated.

The quizzing of the 'plebes', or freshmen (freshpersons, as the world outside West Point would probably call them) is a demanding ritual. There in the open air, on the parade ground, first-year cadets are orally examined by their seniors in anything from the dates of Presidents to the contents of that morning's *New York Times*. I watched it all through my binoculars, and alarming indeed were the attitudes of the examining seniors, touching the responses of the apparently terrified freshmen, as with severe military snap questions were put and answers offered. Sometimes lists of names were demanded. Sometimes they seemed to be reciting poems, or perhaps military regulations. Sometimes songs were compulsorily sung.

'Is that some patriotic ballad?' I asked of a senior cadet, as a not very musical salvo of melody reached me from the other end of the ground. 'Ma'am', he replied (courtesy is endemic at West Point),

'Ma'am, I believe that is the national anthem'—and hardly had he spoken than the band struck up, orders were barked, swords were shouldered, and the whole grey seething mass swarmed up the steps into Washington Hall, where a plain but nourishing lunch awaited it.

Actually they were bellowing, so I later learnt, the second verse of the National Anthem. Everyone knows the first verse, after all, and almost nothing about West Point is easy, or exactly simple. Hanging around the place another time, when the cadets were coming out of class, I noticed that whenever juniors passed badged seniors, they uttered a kind of mantra. What they were saying was this: 'Beat Louisville Sir'—'Beat Louisville Sir'—'Beat Louisville Sir'. Louisville was West Point's next football opponent, and having to remember the fact, and mouth this esoteric spell time and time again as they walked across the campus, was one of the subtle ways in which the Academy brainwashes its recruits.

Brainwashing it undoubtedly is. The West Point System, as it is constantly called (reminding me uncomfortably of the names they used to give especially horrid Victorian methods of penal discipline)—the West Point System presupposes that the new recruit has to be re-created from scratch. All the High School swank has to be scoured, all childish pride expunged, and since this is achieved not by members of the staff, but by the endless harrassing and criticism of cadets only a few years senior, the whole nature of military discipline and hierarchy is experienced. Now you are the unfortunate underdog, now you are in command: you know the bitter trade from both sides.

At the same time the pressure of daily life is merciless, the pace terrific, the standard of everything frighteningly high. A cadet graduates from West Point not only with a science degree, but with a military education both theoretical and practical, and a physique transformed by endless exercise. There is no slouching about on this campus. Everybody moves at a spanking pace, left right, left right, head up, eyes often a bit glazed, generally sunk in thought—trying to remember differential calculi, perhaps, or what the *Times* said that morning about economic conditions in Sumatra.

It is a hard, calculated regime, and some of those plebes look tired enough to wring a mother's heart. Observe though some of their seniors, as they prepare for the afternoon's exercise! Handsome and amiable young giants jog down to the football field. Astonishingly energetic girls do violent aerobics. Sweating toughs lift enoromous weights, throw themselves around exercise bars, or do so many press-ups, with such enthusiasm, that it exhausts me just to watch them. 'Let's go!', cry the coaches, 'Lift those knees!', 'Carry that ball!'—breaking off sometimes to offer me a polite 'Hi' as I meander flabbily past.

I was seeing it only from the outside, but nevertheless I was greatly cheered up by all this. A quarter of West Point's cadets drop out, and I don't blame them, but the ones who survive seem to me just fine. I tried hard to detect symptoms of fraud, hypocrisy or Rambo arrogance in the ones I met, but they seemed to me, to resurrect a phrase, ladies and gentlemen every one. If it is an élite that West Point produces, it is a very attractive élite, and hardly homogenous: there are cadets black, brown and yellow, Jewish cadets, many be-spec-tacled cadets, cadets short and even cadets who look to me a little plump for press-ups. They come from all backgrounds, posh to poor, and the one thing they have in common, so West Point likes to think (me, too) is the devotion instilled to them, during their four years in the place, to principles that the Founding Fathers would have approved of.

I am anything but a militarist—more of a pacifist-anarchist, actually—and I was surprised to find myself, as I pottered around West Point, so attracted by its atmosphere. Partly, of course, it was the contrast between this place of old-school values and the contem-porary squalors outside. Partly perhaps it was the aesthetic appeal of order and tradition, set against the glorious landscape of the Hudson valley. But perhaps it was chiefly a sense of nostalgic *déjà vu*. In the days when we British were masters of the world we too consciously produced an élite to keep it straight, and West Point has a lot in common with the schools that educated the English governing classes. *Mens sana in corpore sano*, a healthy mind in a healthy body—that was their ideal, as it is the Academy's now, and they too liked to suppose that they were educating a band of brothers, united in trust and loyalty, to organize a New World Order, in those days called the Pax Britannica.

Hyped up as I was by these conjectures, West Point never let me relax, just as it never lets the Long Grey Line drop its guard. Everywhere I went trophies and symbolisms prodded me: rows of captured artillery, benches inscribed 'Dignity', 'Perseverance', 'Responsibility', eagles and crossed swords, the flag on a flagpole 140 feet high, the Cadets' Prayer ('guard us against flippancy and irreverence') the Academy motto ('Duty, Honor, Country'), the sundial presented by the Class of '33 ('From its Time and Place in the Long Grey Line'), the vulgar gold and ivory baton surrendered by Reich-Marshal Goering, the very antithesis of a West Pointer, to the forces of Truth in 1945. 'Beat Louisville Sir' mumbled the plebes. 'Duty, Honor, Country', thundered the text around General McArthur's statue. 'To be good officers, you must be good men', said the shade of General Sherman. 'If you admit you're wrong', I heard a coach assure his perspiring footballers, 'you're already right, and you don't get yelled at.'

Best of all, most genuinely inspiring, was a little cameo I saw on my last afternoon at West Point. It was a Saturday, and many of the cadets were preparing to receive visitors, or go out. I saw one vigorous plebe emerging from her barracks in what I took to be her semi-dress uniform—not the famous ceremonial one that we always see in West Point photographs, with the cross-belting and the plumed hat, but a trim grey trouser suit with a shiny-peaked cap, very smart and very flattering (if one may dare say such a thing, in such a context) to her lithe figure.

I followed her down the path towards the Eisenhower statue—left right, left right, head up, arms swinging, brisk as could be to where her father was waiting to meet her: and then—talk about symbolisms! He was your very image of a kindly homespun countryman, a figure from an old magazine cover, wearing boots and a floppy brown hat, his face shining with pride and happiness. She broke into a run, her cap went skew-whiff for a moment, and into his strong American arms she fell.

| V | E | N | I | C | E |

Into the Bar

If there is one place that lives up to the cinematic title of this book, it is certainly Harry's Bar in Venice—a starry institution in perpetual performance. Having loved it all my adult life, I was immensely flattered when its owner, Arrigo Cipriani, invited me to contribute an introduction to the cookery book he was writing, called The Harry's Bar Cookbook. *I know nothing about cooking, and not much about food, so this little essay is what I gave him.*

IT was in 1946, when the war in Europe had hardly ended and Venice was still under the control of the Allied armies, that I first poked my nose through the doors of Harry's Bar in Venice. I was young, rather shy, and extremely unworldly, and I did not know what to expect. From the outside the place hardly looked like a bar, occupying as it did an elegant building like a little palazzo. The frosted glass of its windows made it difficult to peer inside. I had heard tales of vast prices and an excruciatingly grand clientele. My friends, feeling, I suspect, much as I did, pushed me through the door first, sheepishly treading on my heels; but the moment I got inside, adjusting my eyes from the sunshine to the shade, I found myself in thrall.

The room was smallish and unexpectedly cosy. At the tables were smoky-looking, hooded-eyed, tweedy, sometimes hatted, heavily made-up, but rather weather-beaten persons I took to be members of the Italian aristocracy. Sitting at the bar were three or four allied officers, the British looking disconcertingly suave to me, the Americans dauntingly experienced. The conversation level was low but intense, there was a discreet clinking of plates somewhere out of sight, and a solitary ample man at a table by himself was already well into a plate of scampi. Everybody, even the scampi man, looked up as I made my entrance. The officers looked up in a cool, officerlike way, holding their glasses. The patricians looked up patricianly, rather disappointedly, as though they had been hoping for better things. The fat man looked up with his eyes only. But it was the contact I had with the three pairs of eyes behind the counter that I remember best—the eyes of the boss sitting behind his cash till, the eyes of the two busy barmen in their white jackets. The expression in their gaze seemed to me generic to the place. It was at once interested, speculative, faintly amused, and all but collusive. It put me simultaneously at my ease and on my guard, made me feel in some curious way a member of the establishment, and has kept me going back there from that day to this.

Harry's Bar is by now one of the world's most celebrated restaurants, but its style has not changed one iota since I first set foot in it. It is a style altogether *sui generis*, bequeathed by its founder, Giuseppe Cipriani, to his successors and employees, and apparently effortlessly maintained. The very name of the place evokes, not simply a cuisine, or a kind of drink, but a frame of mind.

Some great restaurants live by their formality. Nobody would want it otherwise. There are times in life—very few in my own case, but still occasional—when it seems right for the ambience to be a little inflexible, when a strict code of dress can be forgiven, when napery, cutlery, exquisitely printed menu, slightly patronizing welcome, perceptibly stiff service, the kind of décor that one would rather die than have to live in at home all combine to create, as the guidebooks say, a particular kind of dining experience. One might think that Venice, with its long tradition of aristocratic privilege and its continuing weakness for titles, might be just the city for such institutions. In fact its best restaurants are relatively easy going. I put this down partly to the effects of tourism, which weakens all pretension, but more fundamentally to the effects of history. For a thousand years this was, besides being the capital of an empire, a great mercantile city and a city of the sea. Influxes of Slavs from Dalmatia tempered its Italianness; Jewish bankers helped to give it gravity; in the heyday of the city the ruling aristocracy itself was no tom-fool hierarchy of the idle rich, but a caste of dedicated merchant princes, admirals, and administrators. Coupled with all this were a highly calculated love of ceremony and a gift for publicity. No nation ever presented itself with more panache, confident as the Venetian republic was, almost until the end of its independent history, that it would last forever.

Great restaurants reflect the history of their settings and help to illustrate their meanings. I don't think it fanciful to recognize many of the most profound Venetian traits in the personality of Harry's Bar— the diligence and the craftsmanship, the Slavic strength and the Italian grace, the touch of gravity and the talent for display. Certainly the same bitter-sweet mixture of delights could hardly have evolved anywhere other than Venice.

For more than forty years now, on and off, I have myself looked up from my table to see who is coming through those famous doors. Often the people who enter are familiars of the place—jet-set Venetians, New Yorkers who know everyone, weekenders from Milan, Venetophiles from all over the world who regard a meal or a drink at Harry's Bar as an essential Venetian pleasure. Often, though, they are first-time patrons attracted to the place by the legend of its name, and in their frequently diffident and even apprehensive entrances I see, of course, myself when young. They are expecting that haughty headwaiter, that rigidity of convention inside. Instead they find (unless they are wearing shorts, the one item of dress, I believe, that Harry's does not welcome) that they have fallen among friends. And though there may be a temporary lapse in the euphoria when the newcomer sees the menu prices, I have yet to observe one leaving disgruntled—broke perhaps, but never disgruntled.

This is far more than mere charm. It is professionalism of a particularly delicate kind, and the old Venetians would be as proud of the system at Harry's Bar, I think, as they would be beguiled by its manner and seduced by its food. There is something rather nautical about the way the place is run. It is marine in setting, standing as it does beside the bobbing boats and jetty at the Grand Canal end of the Calle Vallaresso—next door, as it happens, to the offices of the port captain. It is also shiplike in manner. Its two rooms, upstairs and downstairs, feel extremely well stacked. Everything seems in order and neatly piled—shipshape, in fact. The waiters are not unlike stewards, deft and quick on their feet, and the acquaintances that I frequently strike up in Harry's Bar, where it is very easy to fall into conversation with the people at the next table, are very like transient shipboard friendships. If Arrigo Cipriani, the founder's son, is in the house, his presence is very captainly (indeed, he has probably navigated himself to work in his own motor launch).

Then again, Harry's Bar is a bar; it began as one, and it remains one. Napoleon said the Piazza San Marco was the best drawing-room in Europe; I would nominate Harry's as one of the two or three best saloons. It is also a café, offering the very essence of the café society that once played so large a part in the affairs of Europe. It is not that one would normally go into Harry's just for a cup of coffee, though some people do; but the atmosphere of the restaurant, the warm immediacy of it, the company always of people who know each other, the ease of converse, the knowing attitudes of the staff—all these add up to the clublike feeling that all the best cafés possess. I have often sat for hours in a corner of Harry's Bar, working, eating and drinking, watching the people come and go, and I have felt then happily at one with all the myriad poets and novelists, in every European country, who have done their writing in the corners of coffee shops.

I feel anomalously at one, too, with the multitudes of regular customers, now extending into generations, who consider themselves in some sense members of this place. I am by no means a gourmet; I am certainly not a scowling smoky countess or a perigrinating socialite; I sit in the bar generally alone and usually unnoticed. But I have this claim to membership: that long ago, when I was young and innocent, I recognized the look in the eye of Harry's Bar for what it was—the sign of a truly great restaurant, whose atmosphere I can immediately reconjure, wherever I am in the world, simply by imagining myself opening those doors.

| T | E | X | A | S |

Where the Worlds Meet

*I*n the 1980s I wrote a series of articles for the magazine Texas Monthly *in Austin, ending with this piece about the Mexican frontier. All the talk at that time was about illegal immigration and drug smuggling from the south, and every day's paper seemed to carry inside stories about border violence and mayhem. I decided, however, to view the subject in a more general or cowardly way.*

WHICHEVER way you drive down to Presidio you will pass through classic Texas country—scrub-and-desert country, cow country, buck country, where great trains crawl tentatively across mighty landscapes, and ranch houses stand isolated on apparently unreachable horizons. The little towns along the way proclaim themselves very Texanly. Alpine (population: 6,818) claims to be the Biggest Town in the Biggest County in the Biggest State in the United States; Sierra Blanca (altitude: 4,512 feet) says it has the best climate in the world; Marathon boasts of its all-woman chamber of commerce; the masthead of the *Sanderson Times* is embellished with an oil rig, a cowboy, and a railway engine—potent Texas symbols every one.

But when you get into Presidio County, and the road heads southward through the emptiest country of all, everything changes. It gets hotter as the road loses altitude, and the scrub becomes strangely speckled with white-blossoming yuccas. Ahead of you there rise

73

mountains, ribbed and sunbaked. The dust seems dustier somehow. The air is certainly sultrier. And when you enter the town of Presidio itself (population: 2,070; altitude: 2,594 feet), you feel yourself to be hardly in Texas at all.

Presidio is a shabby crouched little town with no brag to it. Its low mud-brick buildings include several bars and hardware stores, a bus station, a notary public's office, and a pair of churches. The streets seem to be more or less abandoned, especially if you arrive in the middle of the day, the houses look clamped, those stark mountains loom rather meanly in the background, and a sense of spooky resignation hangs over everything. Ninety-three degrees is the temperature, and a hot wind blows. Keep going through the town though, and before long you will reach a narrow muddy river, crossed by a rickety pole-shored bridge; and here you may feel a frisson of a different kind.

There are a few huts down there, in the shade of the cottonwood trees, and around them a little crowd of brown-skinned people hangs around, as though they are waiting for something. Two bulky men in uniform survey them, chewing gum and leaning against walls in the shade. Rock music thumps from somewhere. Now and then a car comes plunging down the pot-holed track from the bridge. On the far side of the river two horses on the bank flick their tails in the heat, and beyond them is a huddle of brown houses, and a church tower. You may feel that the scene has something obscurely significant to it, some sense of latent power or historical meaning—something allegorical, perhaps.

And you will be right. That modest river is the Rio Grande, and you have reached one of the earth's archetypal frontiers. On this side is the United States, on that side is Mexico. Here the generic North confronts the notional South, and the richest society on earth comes face to face with the Third World.

There is no pretending that it is a comfortable frontier, or even by and large a beautiful one. The Rio Grande forms the entire southern boundary of Texas, and it runs for about a thousand miles through spectacularly varying terrain—from the great border city of El Paso in the west, commanding the Pass of the North from Old Mexico into New, through remote canyons of Big Bend, past the arable country that Texans call simply the Valley, where the land blossoms into prodigies of fertility and is fallen upon by hordes of elderly Midwesterners in recreational vehicles, to peter out at last in the desolate salt marshes of Boca Chica on the Gulf of Mexico. It is, however, a frontier less than absolute, because thousands upon thousands of people from the south live to the north of it, speaking their own language and preserving more or less their own culture. It reminds me of the place on the beach where the tide turns, leaving behind its long deposit of seaweed, plastic bags, pretty shells, and messages in bottles. Perhaps it is less a frontier really than a kind of no man's land between countries, a transient, blurred, and uncertain place, where you are seldom sure which culture is paramount, which language is more readily understood, or even which nation you are looking at.

Arriving one steamy afternoon at a place called Roma, in Starr County, I felt those cross-bred effects to have reached a bewildering climax. The river there is perhaps a hundred yards across, and very shallow, and on each side is a small town. The two of them seemed to me all but indistinguishable.

I stood upon the Texas bank, but I might just as well have been in Mexico. Whitewashed adobe buildings were on both sides of the stream, on both sides tumbled dwellings hung with washing, snuffled about by pigs and dogs. All was indeterminate and intermingled, and the river seemed less a division than a shared amenity. A cock crowed somewhere, but whether it was a Mexican or an American rooster I could not tell. Someone shouted, but in a throaty indeterminate tongue.

Where was I? I felt I was nowhere in particular, in a frontier limbo. Even as I watched, a small boy on a bicycle rode straight into the river on the Mexico side and splashed merrily across the shallows to a Texas sandbank, raising plumes of spray behind his wheels. When I walked away from the river, back toward US Highway 83, I saw looking out at me from a parked car a swarthy, unsmiling, and dark-spectacled man whom I recognized instantly as a Central American arms salesman, kidnapper, or possible political subversive. 'Adios,' I said as I passed him. 'Have a nice day,' he murmured shyly in reply.

The Tex-Mex frontier is a pungent place. Everything about it is pungent. Here now sits the Reverend Canon Melvin Walker La Follette, head of the Episcopalian mission in Redford, a river hamlet where the customs men, they tell me, prefer to pursue their investigations in pairs, and where clans who have lived here since before Texas was born maintain their immemorial feuds on both sides of the Rio Grande.

The Reverend Canon Melvin Walker La Follette is unperturbed, for he is the very model of a modern frontier priest. Dressed in T-shirt, jeans, and sneakers, he sits amid the indescribable cheerful confusion of his small house (theological treatises and Greek lexicons spilling all over the floor), showing me on a map the immense and mainly roadless area of his parish, across which he pursues his pastoral missions in a hefty four-wheel-drive truck provided by his bishop. He hardly recognizes the existence of the border, helping people indiscriminately on both sides of the river and ministering to anyone who asks, in any language. In the yard he keeps two goats, some chickens, a quarter horse, and a couple of dogs. He looks like a Welsh rugby player and is officially described as Canon Missioner of the Episcopal Diocese of the Rio Grande.

The frontier is rich in such figures, like characters out of fiction, deposited here as miscellaneous flotsam themselves. Such speculations they arouse! By what romantic route did the blond and smiling Swiss lady, like someone out of a Renoir, come to preside over her breakfast counter in Laredo? What brought to this tangled country the man in the coffee shop who speaks six languages, who has a home in France and another in Italy, who spends four months of each year abroad but who feels most at home along this crude border? Or what about the storekeeper of Garciasville, who combines groceries with taxidermy, whose provisions are grimly supervised by owls, deer, armadillos, a wildcat, and a big black bearskin from the Mexican mountains?

Proper frontier faces abound, Indian faces, Spanish faces, nut-brown faces with Mongolian eyes, hunter's faces, rivermen's faces, and one face in particular that like some rare fauna seems to be unique to this territory: a lizardlike face, this one, not quite Hispanic, not quite Anglo either, rather squashed-up brow to chin, with hard, hollow cheeks and deep-set eyes beneath the statutory Stetson—a predatory face, which catching your eye perhaps over a breakfast plate of biscuits and gravy, breaks into a savage but not immediately threatening smile.

Everywhere one catches pungent cameos, too. Here beneath the bridge at Eagle Pass cluster the weird beehive huts of the Kickapoo Indians, made of skins, cardboard, cane, and assorted tacked-up textiles, with tumbledown roofs and Indians sitting stolidly on benches outside them. Here a wild crew of fieldworkers, almost black with sun, cheer and dance when a man stripped to the waist throws a weighted net into an irrigation canal and to everyone's astonishment pulls out a muddy fish. And always, at every crossing, you see the shifting, ceaseless movement of the frontier traffic: long lines of pedestrians, heavy with shopping bags, labouring back and forth, back and forth, across wire-meshed bridge walkways; slow lines of cars which, seen from a distance crossing the great humped bridges at El Paso, glitter brazenly in a shimmer of heat and exhaust fumes— this way perhaps to hock a family heirloom at La American Pawnshop in Laredo, Established 1884, that way to consult Jesús Aguirre, the well-known and by no means expensive dentist of Nuevo Progreso, who Guarantees Satisfaction and for whom No Appointment Is Required.

San Jacinto Plaza in El Paso is the most pungent paradigm of all. I was sitting there one day watching the passing scene—the clusters of Mexican shoppers comparing blenders or cotton lengths, the twos and threes of weathered old men in their wide hats on the benches, the children playing obscure Hispanic games, the blond scrubbed servicemen from Fort Bliss, the man unenthusiastically selling solid silver necklaces from Juárez, the couple of superannuated hippies with their droopy moustaches and fringed shoulder bags—I was sitting there in the sunshine when I heard music from the little podium on the western side of the square.

Two Anglos in long white robes had struck up a hymn. The man had a straggly white beard, and held a thick stave rather taller than himself. The woman held the hymnbook. Solemnly, earnestly, short-sightedly, altogether ignoring the palm-shaded and exotically peopled scene around them, oblivious to the ding-ding and Spanish cry of the ice-cream vendor on his tricycle down the street, they sang an old hymn straight from the heart of traditional Texas—'Nothing but the blood, nothing but the blood of Jesus.' At their feet they had dropped a hand-painted sign: 'Porqué ir al Inferno? Jesus Can Open the Gates of Hell.' Nobody paid them much attention, but some of those lizardy old men, I noticed, tapped their toes to the beat.

When I was there the hand-pulled ferry over the river at Los Ebanos was out of action because of troubles on the frontier—an American anti-drug officer had lately been kidnapped and murdered in Mexico, and the ferry was closed in consequence. The little immigration building was deserted, the ferry barge was tied up at the shore, and in the sleepy heat of the afternoon only the raucous grackles squawked and hooted. On the opposite bank, where a dirt track led to the Mexican village of Diaz Ordaz, I could see the abandoned table of a money-changer beneath a tree labelled 'Cambio'. There was no sign of human life on either side, which suggested to me a frontier closed by war, numbed, boarded up, and ominous.

It is certainly not an easy frontier—never has been. Though the two riparian governments like to make fulsome public gestures of undying amity, in fact this border has seldom been anything but a heap of trouble. Wars, bandit raids, smuggling, kidnappings, illegal entries, skulduggeries of every conceivable kind are fundamental to its ambience, and although the frontier is unfortified, often and again along its length you encounter a structure of embattlement, whether it is one of the little airfields built in the twenties to control the region with blimps or biplanes, or the nineteenth-century mud fort, perched on a bluff outside Presidio, that looks out across the border wilderness for all the world like a fortress on the Khyber.

Wherever you are on the thousand miles of this boundary, you may be quite sure that very close to you somebody, somehow, is violating it. It is a frontier of interminable, uncountable, uncontrollable mayhem and mischief, from the laundering of drug money to the illegal importation of parrots. 'Smuggling's for the single guy,' a resident of Starr County said to me without a blush. 'I gave it up when I married.' 'Listen,' said another, 'I can make $50,000 in a day, easy, just taking one load of dope up to Houston.' Hardly an issue of any local newspaper, hardly a conversation in any café, fails to mention heroin, wetbacks, communist subversion in the south, or coyotes, the scoundrels who prey upon hapless and ignorant illegal aliens. It is a festering frontier. It is a great place for the two parked cars, side by side, all alone in the middle of nowhere, or the sudden silence in the room when a stranger walks in. The men of the Border Patrol are inescapable here, bundling manacled people into vans in downtown city streets, checking for unregistered aliens at roadblocks, sitting among crackling radios beside enormous maps in tall-masted border post. Sometimes, when the tensions of the frontier are especially high, the cars waiting to cross the bridges into Texas queue in their hundreds far back into Mexico, while the customs and immigration officers examine every trunk, every purse, every permit, and every face.

An incomprehensible flow of wealth, an unimaginable flow of people, cross this frontier night and day. A little town like Hidalgo, which looks like a semi-permanent prospectors' settlement, harbours in its banks and exchange houses hundreds of millions of dollars; along the road in San Benito sixty to seventy refugees from El Salvador are habitually shacked up in the dim-lit, crowded bunkhouse of the Casa Oscar Romero, a sanctuary for political refugees. Look at a labouring line of workers in any Rio Grande field (bent over their hoes, in baseball caps and straw hats, like a row of convicts, or perhaps cotton-pickers of the Old South), and the chances are that half of them are illegal aliens from south of the border—it is illegal to be one, but not illegal to employ one.

Behind all the mayhem, of course, ordinary honest communities, happily mixed of race, get on with their lives—farmers and business-men, mayors and Shriners and ladies' leagues. It is difficult to remember the fact, though, so disturbing are the nuances of the frontier, and so dark its cross-currents. Much more characteristic of its sensations, I thought, than any Sunset Mall or Galleria was a place I came across by chance on the riverbank east of Progreso, in Hidalgo County. Until the fifties a frontier bridge was here, but it was swept away by floods, and now nothing is left but the remains of its immigration buildings and a plethora of faded frontier signs. Even the course of the river itself has changed a little, leaving only a soggy cut-off with a dredger high and dry.

There are a few houses nearby, grazed about by goats, guarded by many dogs, but I found this a chill and spooky spot. It seemed full of secrets, and sure enough, one of the neighbours told me that almost every night of the year people from the south clandestinely cross the river there, and creep damp and dripping through the shrubbery into Texas. 'You see that forest there?' the neighbour said, pointing to a confusion of shrubbery beside the water. 'I'll bet you there's people laying there this very minute, waiting for dark, bad men some of them, from far, far away.' I peered at the bushes through my binoculars, hoping to see glints of Russian weaponry, the smoke of marijuana rising, brown faces glaring back at me from among the leaves. All seemed deserted, though. 'Want to go and see? See if there's men there now?' asked my informant helpfully. 'No, thanks,' I said.

*

79

Nevertheless, for one of my temperament, to stand on the northern bank of the Rio Grande and look across to Mexico is not generally a disagreeable experience. Drifting across the river come the unmistakable Third World smells of dust, cooking, and ill-refined petroleum, together with the intoxicating southern sounds of bells, hoots, and fevered music. What stimulations, one feels, must flourish there, what frustrations and injustices too! The very presence of that southern bank, looking often enough so much the same as the northern one, seems to speak of looser morals, freer ways, more bribable officials, less dependable mail deliveries, dirtier streets, better food, hotter sex, more desperate poverty, more horrible prisons, and an altogether better chance of adventure. In short, it offers the frisson of all frontiers everywhere, the frisson of the tantalizingly unfamiliar. And as good and bad are confused in that contemplation, so Texas too is coloured by influences welcome and unwanted from its immense and troublesome southern line.

A few miles from El Paso stands the seventeenth-century mission church of La Purísima at Socorro, built by Spaniards beside the old Royal Way from Mexico City to Santa Fe. With its carved wooden beams and its saints, angels and Madonnas, it is a cask of Hispanicism. It possesses a quality that Anglo Texas seldom honours but that Hispanic Texas, I suspect, well understands—a quality of mystic seclusion. Although the Camino Real long ago became a busy motor road, an insulating hush seems to encapsulate the little building. You can hear doves gurgling outside, and sometimes a goat bleats somewhere. You feel closer not necessarily to God, but to simplicity, which is an aspect of God, perhaps.

Time and again I felt something like that as I wandered through the frontier counties. Whenever I met Hispanics, whether they were descendants of old settlers here or immigrants from the day before yesterday, their responses somehow seemed more natural, less filtered or homogenized, than those of most Anglo Texans. They were more like Americans of an earlier age: after all, who was that boy splashing his bike across the river at Roma but Huck Finn in another incarnation? Perhaps they have not yet been caught in the straitjacket of American education, which so often teaches people to talk by rote or convention? Perhaps they are mellowed by a more ancient civilization, or a more innocent faith?

This has never been a closed frontier, and much of what is Texan is half-Mexican, really. You might say that the southern frontier, no less than the western, has made Texas Texas—many a legendary Texas hero established his reputation in these Rio Grande badlands, and the high swagger of the Texas cowboy was a Spanish swagger first. Today, though, one sometimes feels that this frontier is not merely open but actually disappearing. That mighty tide from the south, swelling out of the other half of the world, is overwhelming it. Far, far north of Presidio the flow has reached, beyond Sanderson, Alpine, and Marathon, which have been bilingual for generations, into the huge Hispanic quarters of San Antonio and Houston, up to Fort Worth and Dallas, and out of Texas altogether into the heartland of the United States.

I thought of the barge tied up at Los Ebanos. It seemed an inadequate response to this colossal momentum. If history is denied a hand-pulled ferry, it will lie low in the shrubs awhile, waiting for night.

Island of Islands

I used to have relatives in Nantucket, and when I first went there in 1953 I stayed with them in one of the island's oldest (but by no means grandest) houses, giving me a picturesquely romanticized view of the place. I never went back until, in 1990, the California magazine Islands *commissioned this essay, and then I found myself responding in a surprisingly proprietorial way to the peerless island and its problems.*

SOME islands are undeniably more insular than others: few seem more absolutely surrounded by water than Nantucket, Massachusetts, on a gusty night of autumn, when the wind blows wild off the open Atlantic and a whiplash rain assaults the waterfront. Then, as the big car ferry from Hyannis cautiously eases itself alongside Steamboat Wharf, and the lights of Nantucket town gleam wetly through the downpour, it feels as though you are arriving somewhere infinitely remote and oceanic, barricaded against all the world by the stormy sea itself.

The ship looms white and humming above the quay. The trucks and cars come rumbling off. There is a gleam of oilskins, a mingled smell of rain, gasoline, salt, and wood smoke from the town. Back-packers stumble off into the night. Pickups are loaded with children and junk. People greet each other as though they have travelled not just the twenty miles from Cape Cod, but a couple of thousand miles from another continent. There is an unmistakable feeling of adventure to the landfall, and no doubting for a moment that this is an island disembarkation. The very air is island air, the shouts in the darkness are island shouts, and the sensations of the sea are all around.

Romantically though I present them, these impressions are just. Nantucket really is islandness epitomized, not just physically but historically, philosophically, emotionally, socially and aesthetically too. Its early settlers included a predominance of Quakers, anxious to put a safe distance between themselves and Massachusetts's mainland Puritans (who, in their Godly way, detested them); it has lived defiantly ever since, generally bucking trends and ignoring odds to preserve its own famously individual character. Its natives are extremely proud of being different. They feed upon their own extraordinary circumstances, long since flavoured by rich additives of legend and anecdote, and they are engaged now as always in an interminable battle to keep Nantucket as thoroughly Nantuckety as it possibly can be.

In this too the island is allegorically insular, for among all geographical kinds, beautiful islands are the most vulnerable to exploitation. Keeping an honourable equilibrium between past and present, between real life and pretence, is the classic challenge facing all such communities today, and nowhere is it taken up more hardily than in Nantucket. For myself I could not help feeling, as I shouldered my own bags on Steamboat Wharf and set off into town, that I was entering some beleaguered sea fortress; so bravely shone the floodlit towers through the rain, so ruggedly cobbled was the street beneath my feet, and so pugnaciously tight-shuttered seemed the glorious old buildings between which I passed damp, wind-blasted, and leaf-scuffling to my inn.

On an empty heath, the very next morning, I stood in brilliant sunshine surveying the entire island. The storm had passed, the wind had dropped, last night's feeling of civic resolution had given way to a lovely calm. Nantucket is about 14 miles long at its longest point, 3½ miles wide at its widest, and most of it is the scrubby heath known here as moorlands. I stood beside a little lake that morning, a thicket of small pines behind my back, and the heath around me was partly dry grassland, like pampas, and partly a prickly wilderness of berry bushes and small scrub oak a foot or two high. The air was brilliantly clear, the silence complete. I felt utterly alone, except for the twitchy birds that, moving low and nervously, as though they were flying below the winds, hopped and scuttled from one patch of scrub to the next.

My horizon was bounded everywhere by the sea, and it was easy to imagine that aeons of ocean winds, perpetually scouring the island, really did keep the birds flying low and the foliage stunted. Nantucket is a horizontal island, nowhere much higher than 100 feet above sea level, and it keeps its secrets hidden in almost imperceptible folds of the landscape, so that when I drove away from that heath I repeatedly discovered surprises.

Across one rise I found a wide tranquil pond with swans, geese, and seagulls loitering on it. Across another, and suddenly there was a sea creek bobbing with boats. There are little hidden forests on Nantucket, and herds of deer, and unsuspected patches of heather. What's this stone fountain at the road's edge, far out in the country-side? Why, it's a memorial to Ben Franklin's mother, Abiah Folger, who was born nearby. Why is this track so unexpectedly well defined? Because it leads to one of the world's largest contiguous cranberry bogs, a great patch of sludge, scrub, and ditching altogether out of sight of the highway.

This is anything but a desert island—you are seldom out of sight of a house, even up there on the moors—but around the edges it has its solitary situations, of the true American kind: long empty beaches with rickety fences and lighthouses, tumbled grassy dunes, or the long sea spit called Coatue, which curves all around the north shore of the island like a sandy rampart, and is a gloriously ornithological, scallopy, four-wheel-drive sort of place, with the statutory lighthouse at one end of it, and one or two dilapidated shacks built by fisherfolk long ago.

I could happily putter about this desultory landscape for weeks, watching the birds, looking out for those deer, or not very hopefully searching for the little salamanders that are also alleged to frequent it. Sooner or later, though, the twin towers of Nantucket town, or the summoning of its bells through the silence, would draw me into town. If country Nantucket is laid-back, patternless, free and easy, urban Nantucket is all decision, all trim and compact order, all of a piece. It is also, as it miraculously happens, perhaps the most exquisitely beautiful little town in North America: a true prodigy of history and architecture—'shut up, belted about,' as Herman Melville said in the most frequently quoted of all Nantucket quotations, 'every way inclosed, surrounded, and made an utter island of by the ocean'.

The beauty of Nantucket town, which has been repeatedly knocked about by destiny, is essentially sturdy. Its homes range from mere shingled cabins to town houses of opulent splendour, but they are nearly all tough and self-reliant structures—island structures, in fact. Reliability rather than grace is their hallmark, and they stand there, street after street, in attitudes of neighbourly but hardly gushing resolution.

Street after crooked street, because although the town has few straggly outskirts, its shape is wonderfully intricate. Around the nexus of its central square (which is just a wider part of Main Street, really) webs of roads and alleys wander away, sometimes briefly falling into symmetry, more often ambling amiably from one intersection to the next, doubling back upon themselves or petering out in bosky culs-de-sac.

It follows that texture rather than form is the chief attraction of this architecturally exemplary seaport. The junction of clapboard, brick, and shingle, the tangle of green foliage that softens every vista, the elaboration of tall brick chimneys, external staircases, porches, roof walks, and verandas, the rich variety of fenestration, the ironwork, the lampposts, the horse-head hitching posts, the multitude of odd conceits like marble slabs, marker stones, memorial plaques, and hanging signs—all this delightful complication is matched by the patterning of the ground itself, which is a mosaic of cobblestones, slabs and brick paving, all fertilized, when the fall winds blow, by the scattered rotting leaves.

Surprises abound here, and serendipitous cameos. A tabby cat, sitting bolt upright outside a tall white house, looks as quaintly out of scale as a cat in a naïve painting. A woman in a hardware store carries a macaw upon her shoulder. A boy plays the flute on Main Street, and when you go to get some cash at the Pacific National Bank of Nantucket (established 1804), they give you an anecdotal cheque-book; each 'cheque' tells a quaint tale of Nantucket, with jolly pictures too.

I know of nowhere more beguiling simply to perambulate, guided by those two towers—the one of South Church (which is gilded in 22-carat gold, against the climate), the other of North Church (whose steeple was hoisted up there by helicopter, after 140 years without one). No traffic lights will delay you as you stroll—there are none in Nantucket—and even the pedestrian crossings are fun to use, since they often consist of stone flags embedded in the cobbles, like stepping-stones across a stream.

Downtown Nantucket is in splendid physical condition, and hardly a house is not worth looking at. There are the grand mansions of nineteenth-century shipowners, gleaming white and portico'd in Greek Revival style, urbanely brick and cupola'd in Colonial Classical. There are the four-square sensible houses of sea captains, parading in a comradely way down Orange Street (where 100 shipmasters are said to have once lived all at the same time). There are the shingled cabins originally inhabited by black seamen, recruited from Cape Verde to man Nantucket's ships. Then there is a not very terrible antique gaol, with a fireplace in one of its cells and more humane toilet arrangements than they have in British prisons to this day, and Swain's Old Mill, which still grinds cornmeal with heroic creakings and groanings of its mechanisms, and the tremendously classical Atheneum library, and sundry churches, meetinghouses, and civic institutions that look precisely as they must have looked a century or more ago.

Much of Nantucket town was destroyed in a fire in 1846, but it was quickly rebuilt, and today there are 800 buildings that predate the American Civil War. The beauty of the place is no more astonishing than the fact of its survival, not as a reconstruction or a pastiche, but just as solid, just as genuine as it was when it was all real.

For no, it is not all exactly real. Its buildings are real, but much of its life is a sort of sham. The smell I like best in Nantucket is the smell of wood smoke I smelled that first windy night; the smell I like least is that dread odour of the tourist age, the gift shop scent, compounded of perfumed candles, soaps, and ribboned sachets—the smell of Collectibles, and bric-à-brac emporia, and all the tinsel merchandising that mass tourism fosters everywhere in the world.

For a century the main function of Nantucket has been looking after visitors of one kind or another. It entered history in the seventeenth century as an agricultural island, hunted and cultivated by the now-vanished Nantucket Indians, farmed by the first English settlers, who were greatly outnumbered by their own sheep. Then in an epic few decades of enterprise it became the whaling capital of the world, its sea hunters extending their range from the offshore Atlantic whaling grounds to the most distant reaches of the oceans, until the name of Nantucket was associated everywhere with bold seamanship and initiative. Nantucket navigators knew the Pacific Ocean better than anyone else (which is why the bank is called Pacific National). They were chartered Nantucket ships from which the tea was thrown overboard at the Boston Tea Party, and it was a Nantucket ship that first took the Stars and Stripes up the Thames to London.

Nantucket got enormously rich on whales, and almost every facet of island life was bound up with the industry. When whaling fell into decline in the mid-nineteenth century the place was half-ruined. The islanders never quite recovered their terrific old flair, and by 1895 a local writer was lamenting that while Nantucket salt had certainly not lost all its savour, 'the old pungency is somewhat abated by modern admixtures'. He was thinking even then of tourism, for it was pleasure travel, if of a particularly rarified kind, that had by then rescued the island's economy.

Steamship travel had introduced rich people to the delights of the Nantucket summer, and enabled them to build upon its shores the ample Victorian holiday retreats that still stand, memorials of a roomier era, encouched in lawns and attended by dainty gazebos around the island. Perhaps, as the man said, they did somewhat abate the pungency, but they scarcely impinged upon the island's hereditary arrangements. A new patrician class adopted Nantucket in the summer months, helpfully bringing heaps of money with it, but it did not supplant the dynasties of Coffins, Folgers, Macys, Starbucks, and Swains who had for so many generations set the style of the place.

Today the admixture is less innocuous. That small company of cultivated *estivants* has been succeeded by a far less homogenous multitude of summer visitors, whose annual assault upon the island sensibilities takes its breath away in season, and leaves it with severe withdrawal symptoms when winter comes. More than half those delectable homes of Nantucket town are left empty out of season; all across the island, houses and condominiums are left locked and boarded from fall to spring, haunted all too often by the cats their owners leave behind. And I am told that when summer returns, and Nantucket's permanent population of some 7,000 is swollen to its seasonal peak of 40,000, permanent gridlock all but seizes the dear old streets of the town.

All the threats that threaten islands are here in epitome. All over the countryside new houses are sprouting, nibbling away at the open moors, dutifully clad in clapboard or shingle but often grossly oblivious to the nature of the land. The first suggestion of a shopping mall has appeared, a cloud no bigger than a man's hand, on the outskirts of Nantucket town. The development companies, the real estate men, the insurance people, the gift shoppe entrepreneurs, the vendors of comical T-shirts, the sellers of scented candles and wooden Latin American parrots have so proliferated that few indeed of the old island stores are left. Most of the waterfront area, now given over to yachts and such, belongs to a big mainland corporation, and a proposed new wharfside development threatens to alter the whole aspect of the port.

'Nice thing about a small town,' I heard one man say to another on Centre Street one day, 'you can do business in the street like this.' But I thought he was either a corporation man himself or was whistling nostalgically in the dark, for there does not seem to me much down-home, small-town, grass-roots feeling to Nantucket commerce any-more, and the cap-à-pie feeling I sensed on Steamboat Wharf that first night, and came increasingly to admire as I got to know the town better—that up-in-arms attitude stems from the resolution of true-blue Nantucketers, whether natives or summer persons, to stop the rot, or at least keep the balance.

Nantucket public manners incline to the offhand, edging away some-times into the surly. Service is by no means always with a smile. Being of charitable disposition, I attribute this to historical osmosis, and like to think it just another symptom of Nantucket's ornery island pride—part of this citizenry's stubborn resistance to everything that might taint or trivialize their island.

For the resistance is inescapable. Hardly a Nantucket conversation does not revert, in the end, to the matter of development and conservation, and hardly an issue is not entangled in controversy, from sewage to fire precautions (the town's fire chief waved to me with particular cheerfulness when we passed in the street one day, and well he might, for he had just been cleared of accepting improper favours from one of those property developers). Not much slips by in this island. The whole of Nantucket town has been declared a National Historic District, and tight rules control the look of buildings, if not always the numbers: about the only thing allowed to jar with the venerable presence of the town are the rickety telegraph poles that still line the streets, and I get the feeling that even they are almost certainly doomed.

A host of institutions, public and private, stands up for the island integrity: the historical association, which has been hard at it for more than ninety years; the conservation foundation, which owns the great cranberry bog; the land bank commission, which administers a tax devoted to the preservation of country areas; the preservation institute, which is compiling a register of every single old building in Nantucket. A third of the island terrain is now in the hands of conservation groups, and a popular fender slogan is NO MOOR HOUSES (but then I LOVE WHALES is ironically another).

Sometimes it all feels a bit too much. For myself I find the suavely lettered NO PARKING signs a little over-fastidious. Occasionally I pine for a slab of vulgar concrete or a gaudy poster on a wall. I would love a roistering pub or two on Main Street, and I shall regret the passing of those homely old telegraph poles. There is an anti-conservation movement too, called People for Nantucket Inc., and one 86-year-old islander, complaining about the strictness of building codes, told me she was thinking of emigrating to the Soviet Union, where she might be more free to do what she liked with her own property.

But she was joking, for she was really Old Nantucket through and through, one of the many women who are among the island's doughtiest champions. In the whaling days the women left at home were obliged to run Nantucket, and in many ways they are still the keepers of its conscience and its functions—the chairman of the Board of Selectmen, the executive director and the president of the Chamber of Commerce, the manager of the airport, and the editor and the publisher of the *Inquirer and Mirror* (established 1821) are women one and all. And it was mostly women who guided me around the defence works of the resistance.

They took me to Edouard Stackpole, for instance, the eminent historian of the whaling industry, who was deep in books and papers at the Peter Folger Museum building. They introduced me to Charles Sayle, Sr., the celebrated carver and ship modeller, who went to sea himself in sailing ships, and who works in a tumultuous treasure trove of ship plans and nautical memorabilia. They sent me out to the Bartletts' Ocean View Farm, where two cows podgily greeted me; for generations the Bartletts have been producing fresh vegetables for the island, and when their produce truck sets out its trays on Main Street each weekday morning, it parks next to a memorial to John H. ('June') Barlett, Jr., who died in 1959 and is portrayed surrounded by animals and vegetables above the lines:

He loved the dawn—
He loved the soil—
He loved mankind—
And all Nantucket loved 'June'

Reality holds its own in Nantucket, if only just. There are people
farming oysters here. There are people dredging scallops in the bay.
There is a working astronomical observatory (its astronomer a woman,
of course). Out on the Bartlett Farm Road Dean and Melissa Long
are making the first commerical wine ever made from Nantucket
grapes. Writers and artists of all categories inhabit the island, from
wishy-washy watercolourists to internationally famous authors. And if
the past is a preoccupation of Nantucket, it is also a living presence,
if only because at the core of the island life descendants of the earliest
settlers thrive to this day.

The miller at Old Mill, for instance, hitching his jeep to the turning
wheel as his predecessors linked their teams of horses, is Richard P.
Swain, two of whose ancestors were among the original ten propriet-
ary families of Nantucket. The Pacific Club is still controlled by
successors of the twenty-four men, almost all retired ships' captains,
who acquired it in the nineteenth century; the club rooms, with their
ship pictures, their whaling mementos, their cribbage champions'
names inscribed on scrimshaw, and their aged players grim over the
card tables in the middle of the morning, would seem perfectly
familiar to old salts of 150 years ago. One Macy may have gone to
New York to make his name famous, but several others are still
around, and the Coffins, whose forebear Tristram Coffin was the
original chief magistrate of Nantucket, are represented by thirty-one
names in the telephone book.

In the old Friends' Burial Ground on Quaker Road, where the
town edges out into the countryside, one gravestone is obscured by a
small bush. I went past it one morning and made a bet with myself
that after a week in Nantucket I would recognize the name upon it. I
was not disappointed. Getting down on my knees to move away the
prickly branches, I was gratified to find it the grave of a Folger—you
know, same as the place where Dr Stackpole works, same as the
Folger Hotel, same as Ben Franklin's ma, same as Charlie Folger the
furniture restorer.

All these people—well, nearly all—are captains in the fight to
maintain the balance of Nantucket, and thus by extrapolation, one

might say, to maintain the balance of all lovely islands everywhere. I found myself, at the end of my stay, downright proud of them— proud, too, of the condition of the island, which if half-ruined in the eyes of its own traditionalists, and fearfully threatened still, is by the standards of the rest of the Western world magically pristine. It pays the price of its fascination in its silly tourist trappings and its somewhat self-conscious aesthetics. It is condemned, like all its peers, to permanent struggle against philistine exploitation and degradation. But despite everything it remains truly one of the most enchanting places on the face of the earth.

Each morning during my time on the island I walked out into the countryside before breakfast, and generally so arranged my itinerary that I re-entered the town down Main Street itself. This seems to me as handsome as any urban thoroughfare anywhere, hardly half a mile long, mostly residential and unostentatious, but nevertheless a street of ceremonial magnificence. Its houses are perfectly proportioned to the thoroughfare, great American elms arch over it, and it bears itself like a structural proclamation of Nantucket's self-esteem.

In the exuberance of those autumn mornings, with the first leafy, woody, smoky fragrances of Nantucket arising, and the first stir of the town around me, I felt almost grandiloquently self-satisfied to be striding down its sidewalk; and indeed I would have strutted clean down the middle of it, like a monarch on some triumphal way, or a whaling master home from the Pacific, were it not that I would almost certainly have tripped over its cobblestones and made a very un-Nantucket fool of myself.

A Reincarnation

*E*verybody wrote about Glasgow in 1990, because the city had been declared Europe's Cultural Capital for that year. I went there, for the New York magazine Travel Holiday, in a spirit of scepticism, having read all too much already of Glasgow's relentless self-publicity, and being determined not to have any wool pulled over my eyes by local patriots. I am not at all sure, rereading this essay now, whether I succeeded in retaining my balance of judgement or not—Glasgow is a very persuasive city.

AY, *well, they talk a lot*, she said in her almost impenetrable Glasgow accent, *but they havna changed much really.* She was one of God's Glaswegians, pawky, tough, stocky, fun, with a face pallid from too much smoking but enlivened by a scatter of freckles around her nose, which gave her a gingery youthful look. I assumed that she was simply expressing a half-serious native scepticism. Everyone knows of course that once-grimy, once-slummy, once-violent old Glasgow has changed a lot—Glasgow's Miles Better, as the celebrated civic slogan has it, Glasgow is Where the Action Is, There's A Lot Glasgowing On. With Barcelona, perhaps, Glasgow is the trendiest city in Europe, gawked at night and day by tourists and travel writers.

Presently I realized, however, that the woman with the freckles was expressing something more profound. We were sitting in adjacent red plastic seats in the concourse of Glasgow Central Station, which is itself a famous example of Glasgow's self-improvement. Everything in that nineteenth-century prodigy is painted and shiny again, with Muzak playing brightly, flower-boxes blooming, a floor of pale terrazzo tiling and a jolly kind of trumpet call to introduce the train announcements. But the longer I looked around me the more it dawned upon me that my companion was right. They hadn't changed much really. They had merely restored a splendid Victorian artefact to its original self, not just in fabric, but in spirit too.

This must have been, I now saw, just how Glasgow Central seemed to its customers a century ago—all this spanking brightness and cockiness. Its heroic glass roof looks brand new. Its intricate forest of iron-girdering seems futuristic still. Not only the fresh-painted woodwork of its restaurants, or the plushy comfort of its Central Hotel, but the sleek gleaming trains, too, lined up yellow and blue at their platforms, the elegant new station delicatessen, even the Muzak and the electronic fanfare—all represented the very essence of Victorian panache. I was experiencing exactly the excitement that my great-grandparents would have experienced, if they had chuffed into Glasgow Central around the time of Queen Victoria's Golden Jubilee. It was not just a face-lift, more a rebirth.

They havna changed much really. What we see in Central Station we see in Glasgow as a whole: a glitzy reincarnation, a city returning to kind, and behaving as it was brought up to behave.

It was old long before Victoria's Golden Jubilee. It was a medieval market, cathedral, and university town, and its port prospered in the tobacco and cotton trades. But it grew into greatness with the British Empire, Victoria's empire of steam, iron, and ships, and in the heyday of the imperial system it was immensely successful. Second City of the British Empire was the catchphrase then. Glasgow's heavy industries exported their products all over the world, its River Clyde was lined with famous shipyards, and its city centre burgeoned into a grand exhibition of Victorian style.

If you think this style was sombre or pompous, come to Glasgow now, where you can see much of it just as it was meant to be, before the smoke of the generations blackened it, and economic decline blunted its assurance. Wherever you look in central Glasgow, festive, buoyant, romantic Victorian architecture greets you. In Glasgow especially it was an architecture of lightness, expressed in a virtuoso use of vistas and cheerful elaborations of every kind. Glass abounds—Glasgow is full of big windows and conservatories—and the skyline is punctuated by fretted and whimsical shapes, with towers like telescopes, and cupolas, and weathervanes, and entertaining bobbles, turrets, and bumps.

It is not all great architecture, heaven knows, but two undeniably great architects did work in Glasgow during the Victorian century—Alexander Thomson in High Victorian times, Charles Rennie Mackintosh at *fin de siècle*. They gave such particular twists to Victorianism that between them they created a unique civic manner, recognizable everywhere in striking fenestration, Art deco ornamentation, curious interpretations of classical modes, touches of the Egyptian and bits of Scottish medievalism. And interacting always with these elements of genius are countless examples of the truest Glasgow building form, the tenement—a low-rise apartment block really, of an especially communal kind, represented in a myriad ashlar and sandstone terraces, crescents, esplanades and winding city streets, and built in reds and creams which, now that the detritus of the industrial age have been removed, turn out to be the real Glasgow colours.

All this has been spectacularly revitalized. Forty years ago the Glasgow presence seemed almost obliterated by decay and dogma. The Empire was lost, the shipyards were closing, the port was moribund, nobody wanted the marvellous steam engines of the North British Locomotive Company. Glasgow's occupation was gone. The city was neglected and impoverished, and when in the 1950s they first tried to revivify the old place, the fashionable sociological theories of the day only made things worse. Acres of traditional tenements were destroyed then, ill-built ugly tower blocks went up around the city perimeter, and the unity of the city was whittled away in loveless housing estate and ill-advised ring road.

Just in time the tide was turned. Refurbishment replaced demolition as social policy. The last of the horrible tower blocks was built (and the first are now being pulled down). Millions of pounds of public and private money was poured into the cleaning up of the city, the cherishing of its arts and the restoration of its old ebullience. If you sail up the Clyde to Glasgow now you still pass mile after mile of dead docks and abandoned shipyards, quays forlorn and derelict, disused cranes, ruined works, broken piles, and overgrown water-steps. Only a couple of shipyards are still at work. Only a lonely Cypriot freighter, perhaps, loads a melancholy cargo of scrap metal, scrunched up there and then from a pile of old cars upon the quay.

But when your boat approaches the city centre, at the famous old landing-stage called Broomielaw, then a palpable sense of vigour and high hopes greets you after all. Old buildings look spruce and confident, new ones sprout up all around. In the city of the shippers and the ironmasters, slinky boutiques, smooth art galleries, discos, clubs and urbane restaurants proliferate. To canned Vivaldi expensively dressed infants throw teddy-bears at one another across the mosaic floor of the elegant Princes Square shopping centre. One evening I went direct from a reception for one of America's most celebrated photographers to a reading by one of Britain's most controversial novelists, and at my favourite Glasgow restaurant (a foliage-filled glass-roofed courtyard in the university quarter) my fellow-diners these days seem to look less like Glaswegians on a night out than delegates to a permanent convention of Milanese fashion designers.

Mind you, the pride had never faltered. Glasgow has always been intensely fond of itself, even in hard times, and more than anywhere else in Britain, has aspired to the condition of a city-State. The freckled woman freely admitted that there was nowhere quite like Glasgow. You know the auld song, don't you?—and she broke into a somewhat tobacco-thickened and screechy soprano—*I'm only a common old working chap, As anyone here can see, But when I've had a couple of drinks on a Saturday, GLASGOW BELONGS TO ME!* There are few cities that have celebrated themselves with such profligate consistency down the years—the bookshops are full of books about Glasgow, the museums are stacked with Glasgow material, there are innumerable songs about Glasgow, countless poems about Glasgow, acres of Glasgow paintings, and more than one bestselling dictionary of the Glasgow dialect.

This is a Victorian phenomenon too. Glasgow shared the powerful nineteenth-century impetus towards municipal government and self-sufficiency. Everywhere City Halls were the prime architectural expressions of this movement, and there is no mistaking the self-esteem of Glasgow's own City Chambers, in George Square, which are rich in all the symbolisms of civic complacency. When the Chambers were completed in 1888 Glasgow's focus moved there from the ancient power-centre of the cathedral and the High Street markets, and to this day the life of the city revolves largely around George Square, which is no Piazza San Marco or Place de la Concorde, but is certainly full of character.

It too has been enthusiastically rejuvenated. At one end stands the towering mass of the Chambers themselves, encrusted with emblematic figures and topped by one of those telescopic towers. The Merchant House at the other end is an ornate palace of monetarism, surmounted on its domed turret by a gilded three-masted ship. The hotel on the north side has lately had a bright new glassy terrace added to it, and on the south a mighty royal crest adds authority to the Italianate General Post Office. There are lawns and trees and ornamental flower-beds, and two supercilious-looking lions, frequently ridden by impertinent children, guard the granite Cenotaph which is Glasgow's memorial to its war dead. All around the square are statues. Some commemorate universal heroes—Walter Scott on a tall central column, Burns and Gladstone and Queen Victoria herself, nonchalantly carrying a sceptre and wearing a crown while riding side-saddle on a horse. Some are of worthies perhaps less exactly remembered—General Sir John Moore, Field-Marshal Lord Clyde, or Thomas Graham the chemist.

And one at least, and that the most telling of the lot, is of somebody most of us have never heard of—James Oswald, MP, whose effigy was erected, its inscription tells us, 'by a few friends'. One feels that the friends are all around there still, for even now George Square has a tight-knit family feel to it, as though all the people sitting on its benches, admiring its flowers, clambering over its Cenotaph lions, are really kith and kin. This is the power of Glasgow, which has sustained it through all hazards. People talk to each other easily on those benches. People share gambles, compare extortionate prices, take their shoes off to give their poor feet a rest. The 5-year-old boy riding his motorized buggy around the benches smiles indiscriminately at us all as he blasts past yet again. His father proudly tells us how much he paid for the machine. Several women raise canny eyebrows at one another, as if to say well, some people ha' more money than sense.

Sitting there among the citizens, looking at those statues, thinking about Mr Oswald and his friends, cursing the buggy-boy, while the big buses slide around the square and the City Chambers look paternalistically down—sitting in this place, at once so old-fashioned

and yet so contemporary, so proud of itself but so neighbourly, once
again I feel time reunited. In my mind I easily reclothe the people in
crinolines and stove-pipe hats, and metamorphose the buses into
horse-drawn trams, the taxis into polished black hansoms, the
chequered caps of the policemen into tall bobbies' helmets, and the
motor-buggy into a mercifully silent hobby-horse.

Ay, well, that's all very well (the freckled woman says), *but life's not
all statues in George Square—and what's a wee bairn doing with a
contraption like that anyway, he'll damage himself in the end.* She is
right again, of course. Life wasn't all statues in Glasgow's Victorian
prime, either, when social contrasts were fearful and many of those
picturesque tenements were among the worst slums in Europe.

I often saw her, as I wandered the city. She was one of those
eyebrow-raisers in the square, of course. She was scrabbling among
the second-hand clothes in the dingy shambles of Paddy's Market.
She was dubiously examining the contents of her purse outside cut-
price stores, and she was for ever hastening, huddled against the
wind in her shabby anorak, along the pot-holed desolate streets of the
Gorbals.

The Gorbals is her home, figuratively if not actually. Forty years
ago the Gorbals was the most famously squalid and dangerous part of
Glasgow, a place where the old tenements had been allowed to decay
into an appalling nadir of misery and sickness, and where the tower
blocks that replaced them had become legends of rubbish-strewn,
graffiti-smeared, crime-ridden disillusionment. In the Gorbals the
woman with the freckles is always visible, hanging out the washing
from loveless balconies, yelling at recalcitrant children, or labouring
home from the supermarket with her shopping-bag (containing frozen
fish-fingers, a can of peas, a tabloid newspaper, two bottles of stout
and a packet of filter-tips . . .)

Much of outer Glasgow, away from the newly glistening city centre
and the lavish western suburbs, remains dismal—nothing like so
luridly poverty-stricken as it once was, but still depressed and
depressing. Unemployment is high. Crime is all too common. Drugs
are easy to get. The vast housing estates of the fifties and sixties,
however imaginatively refurbished, can still seem cruelly inhuman.
They have tried putting post-modernist roofs on the worst of the flat-
topped tower blocks, partly for cosmetic purposes, partly to keep the
damp out, but they still seem grim artificial places, lacking all

spontaneity, lacking sociable shops and good boozy pubs and corners to gossip in.

Yet here is really the pith of Glasgow. 'I'm only a common old working chap', says that song, and nobody will deny that the strength of Glasgow's character, the source of its humour and its comradeship, has always lain in its inimitable and gregarious proletariat—all those freckled women, many of them Irish, with their husbands, and their children, their aunts and their cousins (including dear Hamish in Philadelphia and the one they prefer not to talk about in Australia), multiplied ten thousand times and intensified with each generation for a couple of hundred years. Whether they are punks or municipal officials, wives of layabouts or mothers of scholarship boys, Glasgow's working people are always ready to talk, and always quick with a riposte, a confidence, or an enquiry. I asked a man in a street the way to the police courts, and in no time at all he was giving me a lecture on sea-power in World War II. I paused to tie up my shoe-lace, and two passing women asked how much I had paid for the shoes—far too much, they instantly pronounced. A youth who shared my café table merrily told me about his time in gaol—attempted murder was the charge—and at Paddy's Market several ancient drunks took me aside to assure me, more or less, that Glasgow belonged to them.

Glasgow has traditionally been a staunchly socialist city, a city of the working man, with fierce sectarian rivalries, militant unions, formidable football teams, gang wars, rumbustious saloon and paddle-steamer pleasures. Its poverty has been, in a sense, its strength, binding its people together in the fortitude of hardship, and there is an angry school of thought that says this old tradition is now being betrayed. What is happening to the city, says this line of argument, is a treachery to Glasgow's truest values, and an affront to its heritage. The city is being perverted into a different kind of place altogether, dominated by a different kind of society—yuppified, gentrified, emasculated. That common old working chap is being sold down the drain. The brawny workmen of the old days, who actually made things, are betrayed to the purveyors of advertising slogans, package tours, and imaginary money.

But then can you wonder, in a city with such a history, such a people, that a kind of inverted Luddism pines for the pistons, the turbines, the camaraderie, the mighty ships, the steam, grime, and virility of the past?

*

But it is not so different, after all. Self Help! Free Trade! Full Steam Ahead! These were the slogans of the Victorians, who maintained that prosperity for the great industrialists meant prosperity for the proletariat too. It never did, of course, but the reasoning is the same now, and although Glasgow is still governed by a Labour administration, today as in the old days it breathes the ethos of capitalist opportunism.

The difficulty is that there is no longer any obvious reason why a great city should thrive in the west of Scotland, far from the power centres of the new Europe. On the other hand there is no obvious reason why it shouldn't, either, so the main instrument of revival has been propaganda. A tireless publicity machine has, during the past decade, blazoned Glasgow's merits to the world, and made this not just the Cultural City of Europe, but the Hype City too. Glasgow is a metropolis of brochures, a capital of self-justificatory statistics, and an object lesson in that eminently Victorian virtue, chutzpah.

For the Victorians of course were terrific bluffers and braggarts. There was never an instrument of propaganda like the British Empire in its prime, inculcating not only among its rivals and subjects, but no less among its own people, the conviction that British was inevitably Best. The Glaswegian Victorians presented their city as a very exhibition of brag, glorifying all the achievements that had made Glasgow a true power in the world. 'Let Glasgow Flourish' was the city's abbreviated official motto, but its fuller version was more apposite really—'Lord, let Glasgow Flourish by the Spreading of the Word'.

Glasgow's publicists today have less to boast about, but they are approaching their task in just the same way. As I see it, they are trying to restore the fortunes of their city by sheer will-power. Glasgow's Miles Better because it says it's better. There's a Lot Glasgowing On because Glasgow has willed it so. The theory is that the brazen publicity of it all, if arid in itself, will prove fertile in the end: the livelier, more attractive, more fun the city seems in the eyes of the world, the more prosperity will return to it.

Not that it is all chutzpah. The new Glasgow really does have a lot to offer, and much of it would perfectly satisfy the old Victorians. The vast St Enoch's Centre is the largest glass-covered shopping centre in Europe. The new Burrell Collection, housed in a lovely pavilion in a park, is my favourite museum in the world. The Glasgow manner, that beguiling mixture of power and delicacy, now fecundly permeates everything, in interiors and exteriors, in logos and packagings and the décor of hamburger bars. Many of the tenements have been superbly modernized. The proliferation of art—opera, theatre, symphonic music, ballet, rock, film, literature, painting—reminds me of the days of nineteenth-century patronage, when noble institutions of culture sprang out of the wealth of Empire.

Even the woman with the freckles admits that Glasgow is miles better. She is as fervent a civic patriot as anyone else, and she is as pleased as anyone by the new gusto of the place. It may be half-spurious, it may not have wiped the graffiti off her ghastly tower block or taken her husband from under her feet by finding him a job, but at least it means that when she crosses the river to spend her social security money she is going to a city centre full of life and light and colour. She has been notorious always for her extravagant love of glitter-clothes and ornament, and Glasgow today is just the place for rhinestones.

So the city really has succeeded in recapturing the exuberance of its Victorian past. Can it also recapture the success? The publicists claim, of course, that it is already happening, and that new businesses and service industries are already flocking in, but for myself I prefer to reserve judgement for a decade or two. They talk a lot . . .

In any case one can only admire the bounce of it all, the general readiness to accept change and start afresh. This is very Glasgow too. It was in this city, after all, that the Industrial Age was born, changing the way all great cities lived for ever: down by the Clyde on a spring Sunday in 1765 James Watt first realized the principle of the steam engine. There are a few signs in Glasgow still of the city that this revelation made redundant—a craggy archaic house or two, the stern cathedral, the tough old tower that once marked the city's centre. Most of it, though, Glasgow got rid of without many qualms, eagerly grasping the new order; and most of Glasgow now, I sense, shares in the excitement of today's Post-industrial Revolution.

For that is what we are seeing in Glasgow—a great, famous, and most lovable city in revolution. It is like an experiment with time. If it works, Glasgow may be as thriving a business centre of the new Europe as it was once a booming industrial centre of the British Empire. If it fails—well they havna changed much anyway. They certainly havna changed the popular character, which remains as vivid as ever, or the deeper personality of a city that has remained always, through bad luck and good, through all historical vagaries, so irrepressible and incorrigibly itself.

Would you mind saying that again now? (says the freckled lady caustically, lighting another cigarette). '*Irrepressibly and incorrigibly itself.*' *Well that's a grand wee thing to say about a place, whatever it means.*

Nothing if not Australian

I *was living in Sydney, working on a book about it, when I took time off to drive to Canberra and write this piece for the Hong Kong magazine* Discovery. *Perhaps the contrast between the two cities explains some of my reactions, and excuses the yearning the piece seems to display (now that I reread it) for an element of vulgarity. My tastes are normally decorous.*

I'LL say this for Canberra, the capital of Australia: it is nothing if not Australian. Taking some midday exercise on Mount Ainslie, a wooded bush-land hill rising directly above the city, I was told by passing hikers that four kangaroos had just been sighted down an adjacent track. Along that track I hastened, and found myself deep in the Australian experience. The bush was properly greyish and tangled, gum trees creaked, weird birds scoffed and cackled, ants scurried, flies swarmed, beetles skulked and locusts hopped beneath my feet. Sometimes big red butterflies wavered by, and on the air was an intoxicating smell compounded partly of uknown blossoms, partly of dust, and partly, I assumed, of some pungent indigenous excretion of root or bark. All this, just above the city roofs! I found no kangaroos: but then Australia is a country not so much of fulfilment as of theatrical expectation.

The hill is one of several within the city limits formerly frequented by Aboriginals, who went there every spring to feast on the locally prolific bogong moth. This has always seemed to me a better reason for settling in Canberra than the one which led to the city's foundation in 1909, eight years after the six colonies in Australia became a federation: namely that neither Melbourne nor Sydney, perfectly good cities not far away, would allow the other to be the federal capital. Gigantism, endemic in Australia by the nature of things, overcomes patriots everywhere when it comes to planning national capitals, so inevitably Canberra was imagined on an enormous scale in a terrifically significant setting, on a plain at the foot of the Australian Alps 1,300 feet up and about 100 miles from the sea. From the summit of Mount Ainslie (which the tourist coaches, by the way, impertinently reach without flies or locusts by a paved road up the back) I could see the whole of the Australian Capital Territory laid out before me, and it seemed to have no limits. Geography itself was grandly enlisted, when the original plan of the capital was adopted, so that Canberra seems to be wrapped organically around its hills, and botany was recruited too to clad the site in millions upon millions of trees. The city that lunch-time seemed all but lost in space and green, giving me the uncomfortable fancy that eventually, like some abandoned metropolis of the east, it would all be buried in its own foliage.

The site for Canberra was virtually unpeopled when it was picked for its great destiny. The Aboriginals had been driven off, and most of the land was sheep pasture. The city's shape was conceived, after an international competition, by the American architect Walter Burley Griffin. He saw its focus—the focus of the entire new nation indeed— as a huge equilateral triangle around an artificial lake, with some supreme but unspecified national edifice on a hill at its apex, and the offices and monuments of the federation clustered within its boundary boulevards and along its waterfront. The position of the triangle was determined by the hills around, the lake would be dammed out of the Molonglo River, and the more mundane buildings of the city—its houses and shops and schools and commercial offices—would be excluded from the ceremonial fulcrum.

The execution of this scheme has been almost majestically Australian. Griffin soon withdrew from the project, building nothing himself, and a succession of consultants and procrastinating committees repeatedly modified his plan. It was not until 1927 that the federal legislators moved into Canberra, not until the 1940s that most of the civil servants had arrived, not until 1964 that the lake came into being. Only in the 1980s, after nearly three-quarters of a century, was it finally decided that the federal parliament should be that ceremonial structure at the apex of the triangle—by which time the temporary parliament erected in front of it sixty years before had become a monument in its own right, so that nobody knew what to do with it. Gradually the political centre was surrounded, in the Australian way, by wide patterns of bungalow suburbs; Griffin's central triangle, which he apparently foresaw dense with buildings, was instead developed as a kind of park.

Through it all, nevertheless, the properties of the place were maintained. Canberra was to be above all idealistic, symbolical and preferably symmetrical. Politically it was to be the people's capital, headquarters of the most democratic of all the nations. Socially it was to fulfil the planners' dream of the City Beautiful carried to unexampled extremes. No land was to be privately owned. No development was to be unregulated. No street was to be untreed. For years no alcohol could be sold, no neon signs could flash, house colours were strictly regulated and garden fences were forbidden in the cause of social and visual harmony. Most people loathed it from the start.

Today a quarter of a million live in Canberra, but it remains a sort of urban test case. Can real, lusty life ever be breathed into a town started from scratch for purely political purposes in the middle of nowhere? Can a city dedicated to government, to symbolism, to social progress, ever be much fun? Can an archetypal ideal city really be complete, or does the urban ethos demand elements of congestion and disorder?

Of course a capital requires grandeur, and this Canberra undeniably provides. The axes envisaged by Griffin as the guide marks of his triangle have been honoured. One runs from Parliament Hill, the summit of it all, to the downtown commercial fulcrum. Another crosses the lake, now a large and beautiful body of water named after its inventor, to the Australian War Memorial. The third leads to the cluster of sombre and portentous buildings that house the headquarters of Australia's defence forces. Many a conventional icon of capital status ornaments the ensemble: there is a tall eagle-capped column that commemorates the friendshp of the United States; there is a white carillon tower commemorating the link with Great Britain;

there is a fountain spouting headily out of the lake and the inevitable telecommunications tower with revolving restaurant. The National Library is elegantly columned, the Supreme Court is hefty, the National Art Gallery sprawls beside the water, and sundry offices of diplomacy and bureaucracy loom across shady sidewalks.

Nor have the suburbs betrayed Canberra's presiding ideals. Earlier examples reflected the importance of rank in a bureaucratic city, so that one street might be spacious with top-grade bungalows, embedded in lawns and shaded by fine trees, while another was recognizably more clerkish, its gardens less ample and its verandahs distinctly less suitable for cocktails with first secretaries. More recent suburbs are really satellite towns, scrupulously laid out with shopping centres, parks and all those niceties of social arrangements that progenitors of the garden suburb have been urging for a century or more.

On the face of it there is little to complain about. It is all green and decorous. Griffin's guiding hills are, for the most part, pristine still— genuinely *rus in urbe*. Gracefully winding roads, now and then breaking into traffic circles or subsiding into boulevards, link one quarter ceremoniously with another, converging upon the points of the ceremonial triangle and reaching a climax in the double circuit that surrounds Parliament Hill. The generally unexceptional architecture of it all is enlivened by the unexpected licence given to the embassy quarter, which is an exhibition of world styles—the Irish embassy a sweetly adapted country cottage, the Papuan a tall-gabled spirit house, the Indian a kind of Mogul pavilion, and the Chinese looking like a movie mock-up of the Forbidden City.

Nowadays visitors, especially elderly visitors, generally claim to love Canberra, and there is certainly something restful about it. Nothing is crowded: Canberra is by no means overwhelmed with tourists. Nowhere is noisy. One can stay in absolute quiet, in a green countrified street, within a mile or two of Parliament. No poverty shows. Any squalor is out of sight. Everything in Canberra looks well-fed, well-kept, well-satisfied, and ecologically suitable.

There are some genuinely moving things to be experienced, too. Who could fail to be stirred and saddened by the memories of the Australian War Memorial, honouring all the men who went from this thinly populated country to fight their battles in places as remote, and often as irrelevant, as the Sudan and South Africa, Flanders and Gallipoli, Libya and Vietnam? It was war and its sacrifices that really made a nation of Australia, and for years this was Canberra's one great monument: to stand before it now, and look across the glistening lake to parliament on its hill, is to feel gratitude and relief that a national symbol so tragic should have been overtaken at last by one more full of hope.

The National Art Gallery, though it perhaps has more than its fair share of silly minimalism, demonstrates impressively enough the astonishing range of talent that has emerged from this nation of 16 million souls, represented in the mingled browns, greys, and unexpected mauves that are the true Australian colours, and in names and styles that are known throughout the world. 'Nothing changes, does it?' a stalwart middle-aged Aussie remarked to me, as we inspected Sydney Nolan's celebrated pictures of the bushranger Ned Kelly, depicting him in his grotesque home-made armour fighting it out with the Establishment. 'What do you mean?' I asked. 'Well, there's fellers just like that in Sydney still'—and he said it, I noticed, with pride.

The very fact that this is the national headquarters of a young, virile, and most fascinating Power is itself an excitement. There are times in Australia still, even in the great cities, when one can feel strangely removed from the rest of the world and its preoccupations. Never in Canberra. This is a diplomatic and military town, as well as a political capital, and it is full of foreigners and travellers and assorted international experts. Eavesdropping one evening over dinner at the Hyatt Canberra Hotel—a *soigné* restoration I remember from thirty years ago as the very archetype of the Australian rural hostelry—lingering over my oysters amidst its happy pastiche, I heard from closely neighbouring tables, from voyagers just returned, of current events in Beijing, Prague, Washington, Johannesburg and the Australian scientific base in the Antarctic.

On the other hand . . . One beautiful afternoon in early summer I walked across the great grassy space that lies between Parliament Hill and the lake—the heart of Griffin's triangle—and found that not a single other soul was there: nobody walking, nobody sitting on the grass, nobody having a picnic, nobody jogging, or biking, or consulting their guidebooks, or taking photographs, or making love. Nobody at all in that great space at the heart of a nation but a slightly petulant me.

For one of my tastes, at least, very little in Canberra sets the heart on fire. Its vistas, so green, immense, and symbol-studded, ought to be elevating, but in fact leave me with a dispiriting impression of emptiness, even of disillusionment. For a start it has no sense of continuity. There is no sign of the Aboriginals now (though the bogong moths still come) and little in the place is more than half a century old. Even when I first came to Canberra the lake did not exist. Still more do I miss the social and aesthetic density that is the profoundest purpose of a city—the intimate association of people of all kinds, inhabiting every kind of building, jammed together in din and bustle and misery and joy.

A few miles south-east of Lake Burley Griffin the Capital Territory ends, and just over the border in New South Wales pullulates the distinctly unideal city of Queanbeyan. None of Canberra's restrictions and inhibitions apply there, and driving into its streets gives me a sensation of slightly shame-faced liberation. I should not feel it, I know, but dear me, what an instant if momentary pleasure its frank clutter provides: the telegraph poles all over the place, the frequently pot-holed streets, the satellite dishes, the used-car lots, the petrol stations, the cheerful pubs, the clashing colours, the messy shop fronts, the general air of frank, fallible, and fructifying human energy!

It is an example that Canberra and its planners are always on guard against, and indeed sometimes I feel that the values of Queanbeyan are already threatening the capital, preparatory to seizing it. It is odd but true that in Canberra, with its exhibition streets and exemplary layout, the standard of driving is quite spectacularly populist. It is a fact that among these decorous capital greeneries is conducted Australia's most active porn film industry, distributing its wares to every part of Australia, and contributing handsomely (through a stiff pornography tax) to the capital's revenues. No longer can Canberra citizens safely leave their house doors unlocked, as they did for the first sixty or seventy years: mayhem of every kind is on the increase in this Arcadia, sometimes erupting into unusually bizarre crimes of violence. Who could have guessed during the idealistic days of Canberra's gestation that one day the City Beautiful would offer its guests an ample choice of call girls, not to mention an erotic telephone service? It is as though the place is yearning to break out of its stately trance, up there around the lake, beneath the mountains, to join the world's fandango.

Hope is provided by the new Parliament House. Few Australians have a good word to say for this unusual building, opened on their behalf in the bicentennial year of 1988. Some object to it on principle, as an extravagant display of hubris. Others dislike it aesthetically. But as an unbiased foreigner I find it terrific. I like the look of it, embedded as it is in the flanks of Parliament Hill in rather an Egyptian or Aztec manner, and surmounted by a tripod flagpole flying an Australian flag as big as a double-decker bus. Still more do I like its allegories—and allegory after all is what Canberra has always been about. The first splendour of it is that, though it stands on a thoroughly sovereign site, it is not a residence for a king, a governor-general or even a president, but is the home of a people's assembly almost unique, in my experience, for its free-and-easiness. Anyone may wander with absolute freedom in and out of this palace, watching debates from public galleries, eating lunch at public restaurants, inspecting the myriad works of art that decorate its halls or using the VDU screens that, at the click of a computer mouse, display a generally simpering photograph of any member of the parliament together with his curriculum vitae. Then again the fact that the building is for the most part burrowed within the hill, rather than built on top of it, seems to be robustly appropriate to a nation whose character is moulded so largely by the colossal presence of the land itself.

But chiefly it is an element of showiness that I like about the building—not uplifting, inspirational showiness, such as Canberra is all too familiar with, but something altogether more stagey and flamboyant. From the ground floor of Parliament House we may take an elevator to its roof and survey once again the immensities of Canberra, as we did from the moth-haunted hill. This time, though, there stands above us that monumentally shining flagpole, perhaps the largest and almost certainly the swankiest on Earth, so enormous that when they need to tend its flag they ride up one of its tripod legs in a cable car. And when the time comes to leave, we may do something absolutely stunning, absolutely Australian, and altogether entertaining. We need not take the elevator down again. Instead we may walk out into the sunshine, through the crisp high Canberra air, with the vast Australian space all around us, and swagger all the way down the outside of the roof—all down the grassy sward covering Parliament itself, from the high viewing platform beneath the flagpole to the approach road far below. There is a boldness, a brassiness and a vigour to this extraordinary arrangement that amounts, I think, to a touch of institutional vulgarity: just what Canberra needs.

*

And speaking of vulgarity, while hunting unsuccessfully for those kangaroos in the bush of Mount Ainslie, on the other side of the lake, I felt a sudden need to relieve myself. I was just doing so when I heard a padding and a shoving and a rustling through the bushes. Kangaroos at last? Very nearly. Crashing among the branches, as I was in the very act, a few feet away from me appeared a very large, very bearded, white-shorted, and energetically sweating Australian, doing his daily jog, I suppose, during the luncheon break from his duties as Executive Officer Grade Two in the Department of Inter-Administration.

'Ho, ho, ho,' was all he said as he bounded distinctly roo-like past.

Boss no More

*C*hicago *was my first American city: disembarking in New York one day in 1953, I spent a single night in Manhattan before boarding the Twentieth Century Limited for the Middle West, and next day I was in the Windy City. In those days Chicago was still recognizably the stormy, husky, brawling place that Carl Sandburg had celebrated, 'laughing the laughter of youth, half-naked, sweating', but over the years since then I have watched it at once burgeoning in culture and urbanity, and declining in huskiness and sweat. In every decade I have written an essay about it: this one, commissioned by* Chicago Times Magazine, *describes my Chicago of the 1980s.*

I MAKE it a rule, when climbing a hill at home in Wales, never to look back at the prospect below until I reach the summit; and applying the same principle to my first morning's exercise in Chicago, I kept my eyes resolutely on the ground as I strode towards the North Avenue Beach jetty. While I walked I thought about the city— generically, as it were, and also prospectively, for I had come to write an essay about it.

'What's so special about Chicago?' they had asked me in Europe, when I told them of my purpose, and they spoke for the world at large. Now that the ghost of Capone is more or less laid, now that nobody reads Carl Sandburg, now that Colonel McCormick of the *Tribune* has written his last splenetic editorial and the Twentieth Century Limited rides no more, few foreigners give a thought to Chicago from one year to the next. Some people, when I pressed them for images or associations, wanly suggested Frank Sinatra. Several surmised that the Chicago Symphony Orchestra might have something to do with the city. Wasn't there some funny-looking skyscraper there? Didn't Oscar Wilde write about it? On the whole they probably had notions just as clear about Brisbane or Kiev— clearer about Kiev, because of the chicken.

Were they justified? I wondered about it, narrowly avoiding death by cyclist as I approached the pier, and exchanging greetings with the park attendant clearing last night's quota of trash ('How ya doin'?' 'Absolutely marvellously, thank you.' 'What's that again?'). Did Chicago, 1988, get the recognition it deserved? Where did it stand in the ranks of the cities? Did it possess the attributes of a true metropolis— the style, that is, the personality, the purpose, above all perhaps the symbolism? Meditating thus, I reached the end of the jetty and turned to see the view.

Thump. Laid out there in esplanade before me, Chicago did not look at I expected it to look. I have known this city on and off for thirty-five years, since the days when the now unobtrusive Playboy Building (née Palmolive) was the dominant lakeside structure, and in my own fancy I always think of it as essentially frank, breezy, and stalwart of appearance. Not that morning it wasn't. It looked sullen and enigmatic. Clouds swung around its tallest towers, a haze of heat or exhaust fumes blurred its boulevards, and out in the lake the water-intake cribs, grey and lonely, looked like forts or prison hulks. The long line of waterfront buildings suggested to me a rampart screening forbidden territories behind; the clump of the central skyscrapers did not gleam or glisten, but stood as it were matt, reflecting nothing and giving nothing away. I have seldom seen a less explicit city than Chicago appeared that day, and taking this to be an omen of my task, whistled my way back to breakfast just to keep my literary spirits up.

'How ya doin'?' said the park attendant brightly as I passed him again, for all the world as though we had never met before.

*

Before long the sun came out, and at least the style of Chicago was revealed for assessment. Fairly or unfairly, the style of cities is set by their downtowns, and in Chicago this is truer than anywhere. Chicago's downtown seems to me to constitute, all in all, the best-looking twentieth-century city, the city where contemporary technique has best been matched by artistry, intelligence, and comparatively moderated greed. No doubt about it, if style were the one gauge, Chicago would be among the greatest of all the cities of the world.

In bearing as in much else it shows a taste for the didactic. Having hauled itself up from philistine if not brutal beginnings, from slaughterhouse and hog yard, the city is heavy with universities, museums, and elevating institutions, and even physically it fulfils an educational role. Buildings are seldom just buildings in downtown Chicago, they are Examples, and not a city on Earth, I swear, is so knowledgeably preoccupied with architectural meaning. Where else would a department store include in its advertisements the name of the architect who created it, or a newspaper property section throw in a scholarly exposition of theoretical design?

I love to watch the crowds sauntering the Loop and the Magnificent Mile any sunny Saturday. They are sprinkled with indigenous individualists—wild black youths on bicycles, a street performer or two, a beggar here and there, an elderly bag lady drawing a kind of Cubist Ophelia on the steps of the Pumping Station, ruling her lines with the edge of a five-dollar bill. Mostly, though, they are conventional, well-behaved, wondering crowds, eager pupils enjoying a civics lesson. Not only are they astonishingly clean—I am much the grubbiest person in downtown Chicago—but they appear to be without guile. I imagine them getting up early that morning, in small Indiana towns perhaps, or among the silos of Wisconsin, for the trip to the big city; and from one fancy I extrapolate another, and see their great-grandparents, too, rising early on mornings long ago to begin the epic journey from Poland, Germany or Russia to this model metropolis of the West.

Look at our perspectives, downtown Chicago seems to be telling them. Consider our proportions. Examine the stone from Edinburgh Castle set in the wall of Tribune Tower, contemplate the many sculptures by Great Artists, reflect carefully upon the slogan of the DePaul Loop campus—'Education That Works'. Observe the relative absence of obesity and of rude graffiti—that Message From Your

Local Virgin is generally considered socially acceptable in this day and age. Note the absence of racial tension. How elegant the black ladies shopping at Marshall Field's, State Street, the white ladies shopping at Marshall Field's, North Michigan! How content and amiable the faces of the people! Is it not very proper that the artist drawing the Cubist Ophelia should offer to keep it for you on payment of a suitable deposit? Did we omit to tell you that those horse-drawn carriages are forbidden to operate in temperatures higher than ninety degrees, out of consideration for the animals? Oh excuse me, after you, no, no, you first, in downtown Chicago we pride ourselves upon our manners.

I fantasize, but then in many ways Chicago's downtown is almost too good to be true. It really embraces all the North Shore suburbs, which are no more than extensions of its values. I rented a car one day and drove from McCormick Place to Lake Forest, by way of Evanston, Wilmette and Highland Park. Hardly an ugly thing did I see in all those thirty-odd miles, hardly a sign of poverty or disillusion, from the festive perfection of Grant Park to the immense mock-European mansions in which the richest of the North Shore rich incomprehensibly choose to immolate themselves.

I don't suppose there is another such extended parade of opulence on earth. Nor does it seem, like some lesser exhibitions—like Beverly Hills, California, say, or Palm Beach in Florida—in any way illusory. There is nothing flimsy to the Chicago style. Buildings look built to last here, and so far the place has escaped the worst of Post-Modernist Silly. This is one city of the Western world that has generally been honoured by its architects, and as an aficionado of urbanism I can hardly think of a better residence than one of those beautifully modelled and meticulously constructed pavilions from which the fortunate bridge attendants control the traffic of the Chicago River, surrounded on all sides, as if they were controlling the Ponte Vecchio in Florence, by architectural wonders.

It is the texture that counts—the denseness, the movement of one tower against another, the intricate intervention of the elevated railway, the softening of the street grid by the wayward passage of the river, the curve of the lakeshore, the contrast between the cramped complexity of the Loop and the swagger of North Michigan running away into that privileged suburbia. Though this is a linear downtown, seldom more than a mile deep, it seldom feels confined, and since it does not seem either particularly old, or particularly new, it easily absorbs all manifestations of city life. The London buses that take tourists around its streets, their roofs ripped off for windier viewing, are perfectly at home in this setting; and when, looking out of my window early one morning, I saw several hundred people entering the lake water for the annual triathlon, in a mélange of splashing arms, waving pennants and rowing boats, it suggested to me with perfect propriety either a mass baptism somewhere or something excruciatingly historical in Venice.

I could hardly believe my ears. He said *what*? He said, in public, in 1988—you can't be serious!—that Jewish doctors deliberately injected the AIDS virus into black Chicago babies? Style is to personality as pleasure is to happiness, and it did not take me long to learn that nowadays downtown Chicago is no more than a front for a civic character infinitely less superb and sure of itself.

There was a time, for better or for worse, when Chicago's personality was plain for all to see. Carl Sandburg's Chicago, Colonel McCormick's Chicago, Mayor Daley's Chicago, may have been crude, corrupt, and provincial, but it was unmistakable. It was not merely the mayhem of beloved tradition, it was politicians of practised method, it was burlesque, it was the World's Greatest Newspaper and the Nation's Premier Stockyards and State Street That Great Street and cops who talked out of the corners of their mouths and steel mills and railroads and river bridges opening one after the other to let the freighters through—not to mention tough sentences like this one, written by writers of muscular if gaseous prose. Chicago knew where it stood then. If you went to the opera you saw magnates and dowagers on show; if you went to City Hall you saw political bosses and their henchmen; if you went to Billy Goat's you met writers of muscular prose.

'Everybody in this restaurant', a friend said to me as we dined one evening, 'is half-nostalgic for that Chicago'—and actually, though the city has tried hard to get rid of the old image, it is not quite gone yet. A few men in Chicago still walk the streets chomping cigars. Once I saw a genuine peasant immigrant, in a kerchief. People occasionally talked to me of 'the old country'. There is a Rolls-Royce around with the wonderfully period licence plate MRS 1, and the dapper gentleman often to be seen sunning himself outside the Allerton Hotel is Mr Roland Low, last survivor of the vaudeville act Low, Hite, and

Stanley—'Thanks for stopping, honey,' he said with the old music-hall courtesy when I paused to pay my respects.

There is undeniable nostalgia to the figures of the female traffic cops, puffing their whistles like cigars themselves, their bosoms all but subsumed into their bellies. There is a trace of lost innocence to the WGN radio studio performing in full view of passing pedestrians on North Michigan, reminding us of the days when broadcasting was still a miracle. 'The Commies are coming,' my companion wryly commented, when the practice air raid alarm sounded on Tuesday morning. 'How I miss the whores,' observed a bookseller. 'Used to come in here for paperbacks when business was slack.'

But they are only echoes. Billy Goat's still thrives indeed below Michigan Avenue, and its sign still invites you to Butt In Any Time, but even on a Saturday night I found there few of the bulging literati I had hoped for. The *Chicago Tribune* has been tamed with sweet reason and prettied up with new technology, while the *Sun-Times* never has developed into the whole-hog vulgar tabloid every metropolis needs. The St Lawrence Seaway did not after all turn Chicago into a great ocean seaport, as we were promised; one by one the heavy industries, the Sandburgian industries which made Chicago what it was, have damped their furnaces and demolished their chimneys.

And I was right, when I looked back at the view from the jetty that first day, to see the downtown buildings as rampart. Chicago was always of course on the edge of things, the beginning of the unmapped and limitless West; now its wilderness lies just beyond the sky-scrapers, in the ramshackle neighbourhoods which more truly represent the personality of modern Chicago, and which impress me in 1988 as being in a condition of general grumbling neurosis—vast tracts of public unfulfilment, where black activists can seriously bring medieval accusations against Jewish physicians, and where race seems to face race, class class, in perpetual distrust. It is socially rather than architecturally revealing that in the whole of Chicago, home of the world's highest skyscraper and the tallest residential building too, the average height of structures is two and a half stories—such is the contrast between dominant style and prevailing personality.

Not, after all, that downtown dream! But then Chicago has always been a place of intense social self-consciousness, which is no more than the embryo of segregation. Some male commuters from Lake Forest (no female) come into Chicago each morning in their own private club cars, attached to the rear of an ordinary train. I went to the North Western station one morning to meet them. 'I don't see why not,' said one gentlemanly looking fellow when I asked if I might go aboard the cars, but another more accurately expressed, I fear, the Chicago social spirit. 'Looking for something?' asked this suburbanite in the high nasal accent I associate with particularly reactionary attorneys or faculty pedants, and when I told him I was just admiring the rolling-stock he did not reply, but simply went off muttering to himself and shaking his head, as if to say what's the world coming to, look what the cats bring in these days.

Grubby un-American women trespassing on club cars, Jewish doctors planning genocide, yuppies buying up blue-collar housing, Puerto Ricans encroaching upon Czechs, blacks insisting upon black mayors, whites insisting upon Members Only—all the ramifications of social and ethnic prejudice seem to ensnarl Chicago now, and leave its genius atrophied. 'You've got an easy job' said an elderly Pole when I told him what I was up to. 'People's the same everywhere, just hating each other wherever they are.' One night I went out with a squad car of the Eighteenth District, and cruel indeed were the contrasts between the streets of the Gold Coast (where we circled the residence of the cardinal-archbishop, just in case, though he actually has a resident constable within) and the shambles just up the road that is Cabrini-Green (where we patrolled the bumpy streets, paced the meshed and dim-lit corridors, in what I remember as an hallucination of lounging youths, babies, rock music, and derelict automobiles).

Now and then, as we drove round those unlovely purlieus, I heard odd whistles—signals, the officers said, passed from youth to youth to warn that there were cops around. 'Like wild creatures,' I said, thinking of prairie dogs, which warn each other of predators in just the same way. 'Right,' said one of my cicerones (if they will pardon the expression), 'like monkeys.' But actually their relationship with their black charges, though scarcely affectionate, seemed to me practical enough in a world-weary, rough-and-ready way. Chicago has lived with ethnic bigotries for a long, long time. I experienced no trace of racial ill-will myself—indeed I experienced no ill-will at all, except from the man on the club car and the woman at the car rental office, and they hardly count. As I puttered about the incoherent neighbourhoods of the south and west, and through the kaleidoscopic jumbles of Uptown and Rogers Park, I found it hard to imagine that all the dread things I had been told about, the gang wars and the intimidations and the murders and the graft, really happened out there, or that some of those nondescript ordinary streets might actually be dangerous to walk along.

It did not feel a dangerous city, not even when I visited the Criminal Courts over in South Lawndale. I always go to the courts, wherever I am in the world, and was astonished to find these so clean, orderly, and apparently good-tempered: only the glass partitions separating spectators from participants, like the bullet-proof cubicle that isolated Eichmann from his judges, reminded me that I was surrounded in fact by drug dealers, thugs and extortioners. Most of them looked like quite pleasant people to me, but when during a recess I remarked upon this unexpected sensation to a black man sitting beside me in the courtroom, he did not even bother to reply, merely patting my hand with a mirthless laugh.

If Chicago's more deprived quarters reminded me of anywhere, it was of the Old South in its pre-King days. People talked in the high-pitched stylized way that I remember from the Mississippi of my youth, and even in the worst parts the sights and sounds seemed to me for the most part less vicious or tragic than resigned. Here a couple of women, hair in curlers, sit talking and sewing on a porch. Here a very small boy passes the hours away by banging rhythmically on a bicycle horn. A bank has been turned into The True Vine of Holiness Church—'There's Nothing Too Hard for God.' When I meet a man with a very fierce-looking dog, he says, just as might have been said in Vicksburg long ago: 'His name's Midnight. He's a real mean dog. He's gettin' old now, but when he was younger he'd be right up there in that car of yours, right up there through that window. I keep this steel rod here just to keep him quiet.'

Gone are the fetid nineteenth-century slums which took me aback when I first came to this city. Instead it is only a swathe of dinginess, compounded by the remains of dead industries, that lies beyond the frontier of the downtown skyscrapers. An element of the gloomy is endemic to Chicago—even the posh North Shore suburbs can be very depressing in their dark brick and pretension, and the lake itself, when the light is wrong, is a very image of melancholy. So the dispirited neighbourhoods of the poor at least honour a tradition. Little out there looks really terrible, by the standards of the Third World or the Bronx—the misguided high-rise housing projects at least have grass of sorts around them, and there are whole areas of black and Hispanic working-class housing in which, while a Lake Forest commuter might shudder to contemplate residence there, young people from Cardiff to Bangkok would feel themselves lucky to get a mortgage.

I asked my neighbour at the Criminal Courts, since he did not seem to have any oversanguine view of human nature, if he considered Chicago to be in an explosive condition. 'I'll tell you,' he replied. 'It's explosive all right, but it won't light up by spontaneous combustion.' I respected his judgement. It had been a long, hot summer in Chicago, but I felt no clamped-down organic violence in the air, such as I have felt in parts of Miami or Los Angeles. It was malaise, not menace, that I sensed. 'Look at us!' the downtown buildings exclaim. 'Where are we heading?' querulously enquire the rambling potholed neighbourhoods.

Was there ever a name more full of purpose than Chicago's? Europeans pronounce it as if it were spelled Chickargo, which gives it a slightly prissy feel, but spoken as Chicagoans themselves speak it, with a bit of a spit to give heft to its slither, it is gloriously onomatopoeic. Some cities are born by the accidents of history, but Chicago was on purpose from the start—consciously the great outpost of the New World, maturing as the years passed into the great junction and the great manufactory too. All railroads led to Chicago, and only yesterday, it seems, an airline map of North America showed the great black blobs of Midway and O'Hare utterly dominating the interior.

Chicago used to be proudly aloof to the anxieties of the great world, and even now, for all its high fashion and trendy street cafés, it sometimes feels far from cosmopolitan. Those cafés still somehow seem an affectation, and provincial indeed can be the ambiance of an old-school carriage-trade Chicago restaurant, with its preposterously French French waiters and its parties of four turning up slightly pissed and dying for a smoke between courses. On the corner of Lake and Wabash one morning I noticed a sudden healthy smell of manure; and though in fact it was only the mounted police changing shifts and sweeping their horse droppings out of sight, for a moment it made me feel I was back in the Chicago of the stockyards, which had no truck with fancy foreign notions, and would give that King of England a good punch on the nose, if he ever ventured into the Loop.

But the bragging self-sufficiency of purpose has gone, and today I find it hard to know just what Chicago is for. Like many another industrial city of the Western world, it is in the process of changing gear—stick-shift. I observe that the phrase Second City is less bandied about than it used to be, and perhaps that is because all contests are off. Second to what? Second to Toronto? This city does not figure on the financial circuit which runs the world, from Tokyo by way of Hong Kong, Zurich, and London to New York, or on the social circuit that takes in Paris and Los Angeles, or on the diplomatic progress of the capitals. I cannot offhand think of any Chicago product that makes its way to my corner of Europe, except *Playboy* and *Encyclopaedia Britannica*. The opinions of the Chicago press are rarely quoted internationally. Chicago is no longer noticeably on the way to anywhere else, unless you travel by train, and it is a piquant sign of the times that Chicago locomotive engineers are restrained by law from blowing their horns at street crossings—restrained from blowing a railroad horn, in Chicago!

The hog boss finds his occupation's gone. Paradoxically, for a city built so frankly upon brawn, Chicago's most obvious assets now are its formidable intellectual resources, which are inescapable. This is a very clever place indeed. Intellectuals of daunting power are strewn like germinators through the institutions of Chicago, and internationally famous experts of wide variety work out of this remote inland city: Nobel Prize winners by the dozen, whiz kids of the futures markets, one of the most celebrated of contemporary novelists, one of the most cherished of all agony aunts, the designer of the largest pleasure yacht ever built in America, Alonzo Haney III, 18-year-old chairman of Haney Manufacturing Industries, who is planning imminently to sweep the world with a patented windshield wiper of his own invention. It is a city of musicians and musicologists, whether they be virtuosi of the Chicago Symphony, limpid pianists of the cocktail bars or the editors of the University of Chicago Press, who are even now producing the definitive edition of Verdi. It is also a city of venerable department stores and skilled craftsmen and commodity specialists, like Iwan Ries the pipe people, for instance, whose bewildering range of tobaccos, pipes, pouches, and moustache combs is now supplemented by the Ultimate Pipe Video—'the sights and sounds of pipe smoking hosted by a noted pipe authority'.

These are people of substance, people in the Chicago tradition. But round them more amorphously proliferate the activists of the service industries, upon whom they say the city's fortunes now chiefly depend—whose weapons are trend and publicity, whose clubs are those neo-continental cafés, and whose world-wide effect is gentrification. All over Chicago I hear the tread of service industries, industries without products, without visible means of support, clambering over the ruins of steel mills and foundries, and taking with them, like armies of occupation, the divisions of the upwardly mobile. There is something profoundly moving to the spectacle of Chicago's working-class neighbourhoods fighting, for reasons honourable and shameless, blind or perceptive, to preserve their identities and their ways of life against the onslaughts of mall and condominium—even the bereft inhabitants of Cabrini-Green, I am assured, are preparing to resist eviction when the advance guard of the developers comes scouting through their profitably sited desolation.

So I seem to see the city, so clever but so unsure, groping for new commissions. Whatever it achieves, whether by the intensification of downtown or the rejuvenation of the neighbourhoods, it can never be the same again, never be Sandburg's City of the Big Shoulders, and sometimes indeed I can imagine it all wasted and forlorn: like the seaport of some crumbled Empire, perhaps, left high and dry without a hinterland—like Trieste, whose trains no longer come down from Vienna, or Shanghai in the days when Maoism robbed it of a role. In such despondent moments Chicago seems to me too big for itself, and I imagine it half-emptied by decline, the stately apartments of the lakeshore hung with washing on their balconies, pot-holes all down the Magnificent Mile and children black, brown, and white too shaking their plastic begging cups at the intersections.

Of course it will never happen. The accumulated charge of Chicago is too powerful for collapse, and though the empire that was the American Middle West has lost its cohesive mass, still the energies and appetites of many million Americans find the focus of their fulfilment where State Street crosses Madison.

More than anything, in Chicago '88, I have missed a presiding symbolism. Sitting at one of those street cafés one evening, served my glass of chardonnay by a waiter apparently straight from Key West in the sixties, I could not help wondering what the old mayors of Chicago might have thought of it. White wine and gay service in the very shadow of the El! They would never have stomached it, and nor would the city itself in their day; for those all-powerful grandees, whatever their merits, were themselves Chicago, living exemplars of its public tastes and standards. Surrounded by the praetorian guards of their corrupt political machines, set against the massed ranks of the great financiers and industrialists, the befurred and diamonded benefactresses of art and culture, they provided the city with symbolisms enough.

Like it or not, we all knew about Chicago then, even in Wales. We knew of it as the very essence of America. New York was New York, Los Angeles was Hollywood, San Francisco was the Golden Gate, New Orleans was jazz, Boston was beans and Brahmins, but Chicago was the heart of America in all its strength, violence, avarice, homeliness and absurdity. Remember that old cartoon character of your standard American, in his loud shirt and his horn-rimmed spectacles, wearing a Stetson very likely and mouthing comic but benevolent platitudes? If you asked almost anyone in the Western world where his hometown was, ten to one they'd have guessed Chicago.

Now not only has the cartoon figure disappeared, to be replaced in the world's papers by stereotypes less engaging, but the very idea of that America is forgotten. With it has gone the symbolism of Chicago. To me the city always felt like an American city-state, self-sufficient, like a Venice or a Hamburg long ago—H. L. Mencken called it a Palatinate. For all its crimes and rivalries, it used to project to outsiders a powerful sense of family, and it presided massively over the fortunes (and misfortunes) of its own invented dependency, Chicagoland. Today it seems to me like a republic without a flag, a family dispersed, and an estate without a manager.

It is one of the peculiarities of the city that for all the splendour of its parks and vistas, it has no real ceremonial centre. In 1909 Daniel Burnham the town planner conceived of one which would have formed as powerful a fulcrum for Chicago's loyalties as St Peter's provides for Rome—a gigantically domed civic centre at Halsted and Congress, looking towards the lake across a vast plaza, two railroad stations, a colossal new Field Museum, and the twin piers of an enormous harbour. At least nobody could have mistaken this grandiose arrangement for anywhere else, or misinterpreted its symbolism—it was to be the crown and celebration of the Greatest City in the United States, very likely in the world. Hitler would have loved it, and it would certainly have found its way on to the world's travel posters.

As it is, Chicago, the most superbly designed of modern cities, has no Empire State Building, no Tower Bridge, no Eiffel Tower, no harbourside Opera House, not even a statue of a little boy peeing, to emblazon its identity upon the consciousness of the world. Even Chicago's celebrated self-regard, itself a kind of metaphysical monument, has inevitably lost its power. Nobody would now greet a foreign visitor, as one nineteenth-century visitor was greeted by a train conductor, with the words: 'Sir, you are entering the Boss City of the Universe.' Michigan Avenue is patently not, as Burnham forecast it would be in 1909, the busiest highway on earth. It is no longer true, as Henry Justin Smith declared in 1919, that 'only in the most indifferent does Chicago fail to awaken an ardent curiosity'. The Second City is irrevocably second at best, and for the moment at least the fine old place seems to lack that most traditionally Chicagoan of qualities, punch.

So the omens were correct, when I took the opening walk of this essay: though the cityscape soon resumed its habitual forceful clarity, the contemporary nature of the place remained, through all my wanderings and conversations, only the more obscure. Its old meanings lost, its purposes hazed, its personality somehow disintegrated—only is terrific style, among my criteria for civic supremacy, remains unchallengeable. I was impressed, of course—who but the most indifferent could fail to be?—touched, refreshed, even soothed by some aspects of Chicago. I realized that given that pad in the Wabash Avenue bridge tower I could easily learn to love it. But I seldom quite felt the thrilling frisson of mingled awe, exhilaration, and compassion that is the gift of the very greatest cities.

Loyal as I try to be to everyone's traditions, I left Chicago by train. The Lake Shore Limited is no Twentieth Century, but at least it pulled out of Union Station by the old route, and took me with an authentic clanking of points and rattle of sleeping-car fittings (though not a single toot of the horn) down the South Shore towards Indiana and the East. As we turned the corner of the lake in the gathering dusk I looked back at the towers of Chicago, once more brooding beneath a pall of dark cloud, and felt a pang of remorse at my half-heartedness or lack of faith. But I have to admit that I detected a heretical excitement to the music of the wheels, even before we were out of the city limits. New York tomorrow! they seemed to be exulting, the cads. Back to the known world!

Thwack!

*S*t John's, Newfoundland, is one of my favourite cities anywhere, and no assignment has ever given me more fun than the one from the magazine Saturday Night, *of Toronto, which gave birth to this essay.*

THWACK! Despite it all, the personality of St John's, Newfoundland, hits you like a smack in the face with a dried cod, enthusiastically administered by its citizenry.

The moment you arrive they take you up Signal Hill, high above the harbour, where winds howl, unused artillery lies morose in its emplacements, and far below the ships come and go through the rock gap of the Narrows. Within an hour or two they are feeding you seal-flipper pie, roast caribou, patridgeberries, or salt cod lubricated with port fat. They introduce you to the mayor, John 'Rags' Murphy. They show you the grave of the last Beaothuk Indian and the carcass of the final Newfoundland wolf. They remind you that they, alone in continental North America, live three and a half hours behind Greenwich Mean Time.

They chill you with tales of the corpses lying in Deadman's Pond. They warm you up with Cabot Tower rum. They take you to the site of the city's first (hand-operated) traffic signal. They show you the house into which the prime minister of Newfoundland escaped from a lynch mob in 1932, and the field from which the aviators Harry G. Hawker and Kenneth Mackenzie-Grieve unfortunately failed to cross the Atlantic in 1919. They guide you down higgledy-piggledy streets of grey, green, yellow and purple clapboard. They explain to you in detail the inequities of the 1948 Confederation referendums. They tell you repeatedly about their cousins in Boston, and involve you in spontaneous and often incomprehensible conversations on street corners.

Such is the nature of this city: windy, fishy, anecdotal, proud, weather-beaten, quirky, obliging, ornery, and fun.

I start with 'despite it all', because St John's is undeniably a knocked-about sort of town. Economic lumps and political hammerings, tragedies at sea, sectarian bigotries, riots, fires, poverty and unemployment—all have taken their toll, and make the little city feel a trifle punch-drunk.

The very look of it is bruised. The outskirts of St John's are much like the purlieus of many another North American city—malls, car dealers, airport, duplexes, a big modern university—but its downtown is bumpily unique. Set around the dramatically fjord-like harbour, overlooked by oil tanks and fort-crowned heights but dominated by the twin towers of the Catholic basilica, its chunky wooden streets clamber up and down the civic hills with a kind of throwaway picturesqueness, suggesting to me sometimes a primitive San Francisco, sometimes Bergen in Norway, occasionally China, and often an Ireland of long ago.

'Either it's the Fountain of Youth,' said a dockyard worker when I asked him about a peculiarly bubbling sort of whirlpool in the harbour, 'or it's the sewage outlet.' St John's is nothing if not down-to-earth. The shambled slums I remember from twenty-five years ago have been miraculously abolished, but the best efforts of the conservationists have not deprived the town of its innate fishermen's fustian. The most enlightened restoration of its streets has not managed to make it self-conscious. The first dread fancy lampposts and ornamental bollards, the first whiff of novelty-shop sachets, the arrival on the waterfront of that most ludicrously incongruous architectural cliché, mirror-glass—even the presence of Peek-a-Boutique in the premises of the former Murray fishery depot—have so far failed to make St John's feel in the least chichi. It remains that rarity of the Age of Collectables, an ancient seaport that seems more or less real.

I hear some expostulations, nevertheless. 'Fishermen's fustian', indeed! For all their hospitality, I get the sensation that the inhabitants of St John's may prove prickly people to write about, and there is a prejudice I am told among some of the grander St John's persons (we can no longer, I suppose, call them St John's men) against the city's association wih the fish trade.

Yet even the loftiest burghers' wives could hardly claim that this is a very sophisticated place. It is like a family city, meshed with internecine plot, but still somewhat reluctantly united by blood, history, and common experience. It is the poorest of the Canadian capitals; it has little industry and few great monuments; its responses are those of a permanently beleaguered seaport on a North Atlantic island—which is to say, responses altogether its own.

Actually within the city limits of St John's there are pockets of the probably spurious Arcadianism that Newfoundland picture postcards so love to show. Small wooden houses speckle seabluffs, dogs lie insensate in the middle of steep lanes, and here and there one may still see the fish stretched out to dry, as they have been stretched for 400 years, on the wooden flakes of tradition. Almost within sight of Peek-a-Boutique I met a hunter going off to the hills in search of partridge, buckling his cartridge belt around him, hoisting his gun on his shoulder, just like a pioneer in an old print. And immediately outside the windows of one of the city's fancier restaurants ('Step Back in Tyme to Dine') one may contemplate over one's cods' tongues the whole rickety, stilted, bobbing, sea-booted, genial muddle that is the classic image of maritime Newfoundland.

It really is a community of cousins, too. I happened to notice on a monument one day that the now defunct police force called the Newfoundland Rangers numbered, among its Guzzwells, Stucklesses, and Snelgroves, a disproportionate number of Noseworthys. So I looked up that clan in the St John's telephone book: 305 are listed, by my count, including Randy Noseworthy, Ethel Noseworthy, Dwayne Noseworthy, Franklin Noseworthy, Major H. Noseworthy, and Noseworthy, Keating, Howard and Kung, Accountants—their names constituting in themselves, I thought, a proper register of St John's social consciousness.

It happened that while I was in town St John's was celebrating its centenary as a municipality with what it called a Soirée—generally pronounced swarr-ee, and recalling a favourite old Newfoundland song:

> There was birch rine, tar twine,
> Cherry wine and turpentine,

Jowls and cavalances, ginger beer and tea,
Pig's feet, cat's meat, dumplings boiled in a sheet,
Dandelion and crackies' teeth at the Kelligrews's Soirée . . .

The festivities closed with a public party at the St John's Memorial Stadium that powerfully reinforced the family illusion, and suggested to me indeed an enormous country wedding—everyone someone else's in-law, everyone ready to talk, with no pretence and no pretension either. Noseworthys were numerous, I do not doubt, and Kelligrews were certainly there in force, though content no longer with ginger beer and tea. Jigs and folk-songs sounded from the stage, miscellaneous bigwigs sat stared-at in the middle like rich out-of-town relatives, and when people seemed slow to dance jolly Mayor Murphy took the floor alone, offering free booze coupons to any who would join him—'You have to get them half-tight,' he remarked, as he handed out these inducements, jigging the while himself.

The pubs of St John's are mostly less than trendy. The downtown corner store flourishes. The *Evening Telegram* carries not merely death announcements but long and sometimes extremely gloomy poems to go with them, such as:

He's gone, oh gone for ever,
The one we loved the best.
Our days of joy are ended
As the sun sets in the west.

'Your mouths are so big they could fit in a zoo,' a member of the city council told his colleagues in plenary session during my stay. 'You're a sook,' responded the deputy mayor.

I puzzled, as every stranger must, about the mingled origins of this pungent civic character, and the first strain I identified was undoubtedly the Irish. The simplicity of St John's is streaked, I came to sense, with a particularly Irish reproach, wit, and irony—sometimes I felt that Ireland itself was only just out of sight through that harbour entrance. The prickly pensioners and layabouts who hang around on Water Street, 'The Oldest Continuously Occupied Street in North America', look pure Cork or Wexford. The instant response that one gets from nearly everyone is Ireland all over. And the complex of buildings that surrounds the basilica of St John the Baptist, episcopal, conventual, didactic, societal buildings, is a reminder that here Irish values and memories, however dominant the British colonial establishment of the place, proved always inextinguishable.

126

But that establishment too still flies its flags—literally, for at city hall they flaunt not only the ensigns of the city, the province, and the Confederation but actually the Union Jack too, for reasons defined for me as 'purely sentimental'. This was a self-governing British possession within my own lifetime, after all (no school stamp collection of my childhood was complete without the 1c. Caribou of our oldest colony), and within the city centre it is still easy enough to descry the old power structure of the Pax Britannica. The governor's mansion is recognizably the social fulcrum that it was in every British colony. The garrison church is spick-and-span. The restoration of the Anglican cathedral is authentically unfinished, as with all the best Anglican cathedrals of the Empire. The old colonial legislature is properly pillared and stately, and down the hill is the Supreme Court building, smelling of warm wood and depositions in triplicate, which once also housed the prime minister's office, responsible directly to the Crown in London.

Indeed, as a sign reminds us on the waterfront, The British Empire Began Here—when Sir Humphrey Gilbert established the first permanent settlement of New Founde Land in 1583. The city is appropriately rich in heroic memorials, commemorative plaques, royally planted trees or dukely laid foundation stones (though as a matter of fact, St John's being St John's, the stone laid by the Duke of Connaught in Bowring Park in 1914 turns out to be the thriftily recycled headstone of a dog's grave). Kipling himself worded the plaque at the site of Gilbert's landing, Field Marshal Earl Haig unveiled the Water Street war memorial. Nor are the imperial loyalties merely lapidary: one devoted monarchist drives around town with British flags stuck on her trunk and flying from her radio aerial, and another was not much pleased, I fear, when I suggested that in Britain itself royalism, like cigarette smoking, was primarily a lower-middle-class enthusiasm . . .

'Not that the British', even these zealots are quite likely to say, 'ever did much for Newfoundland.' On the contrary, the general view seems to be that London behaved as negligently towards its oldest colony as Ottawa does to its youngest province. Most people I asked said that emotionally at least they would prefer to enjoy the independence signed away to Canada in 1949, but a good many told me that if they had the choice they would opt for union with the US.

This did not surprise me. In some ways St John's is very American. It does not feel to me in the least like Canada, being altogether too uninhibited, but I can conceive of it as a half-Irish, half-Empire-Loyalist backwater of New England. A century ago the Newfoundlanders were all for free trade with the Americans, at least, and would have got it if the British government had not intervened; today half the people I met seemed to have American connections of some kind or another, mostly in Boston. When I suggested to one elderly lady that closer links with the United States might in the end mean more corruption, exploitation, and general degradation, she seemed quite affronted. 'That's only the fringe of things down there,' she said.

But I looked her in the face as she said this, and I rather think I detected in it, through the patina of the years, the bright eager features of a GI groupie of long ago. I know of nowhere in the world where the American soldiers of the Second World War are remembered with such affection, or where, perhaps as a result, the equivocal colossus of the south seems to be given the benefit of so many doubts. 'I can assure you that at heart the Americans are very good people,' my informant firmly added, and as we parted I swear I heard, as in historic echo, a giggle in the shadows of McMurdo's Lane, and a distant beat of 'In the Mood'.

These varied inheritances and associations save St John's from any suggestion of provincialism. History does it, one might say. The fateful gap of the Narrows is like a door upon a world far wider than Canada itself, while the city's particular kinds of expertise, to do with ships, and fish, and ice, and seals, and perilous navigations, make it a place beyond condescension. Memorial University of Newfoundland has a formidable reputation, the Marine Institute is world-famous, and ships of many nations and many kinds, perpetually coming and going through the harbour, give the town a cosmopolitan strength—rust-streaked fishing vessels from the deep Atlantic grounds, bulking coastguard ships, coastal freighters, ocean research vessels, container ships and warships and ships bringing salt for the winter roads—ships in such ceaseless progress that each morning of my stay, when I walked down to the waterfront before breakfast, I found that some new craft had come out of the night like a messenger while I slept.

The historical continuity of St John's, too, allows it a status beyond its size. The Grand Banks, which brought the first Europeans to these parts, still figure inescapably in its affairs, and the matter of the 200-mile fishing limit profoundly affects not only the economy of the port but its very style. Gone, like enemy aliens from a land at war, are the

Iberian fishermen who used to bring a Latin emollient of wine and lantern light to this northern waterfront, but the statue of Our Lady of Fatima in the basilica, presented by grateful Portuguese mariners in 1955, pointedly remembers still the long Romance connection.

Then the matter of St Pierre-Miquelon, St John's own foreign-relations issue, is really a last irritant from the Seven Years War, which ended in this very city 227 years ago. Though the islands are familiar enough to St John's people (university students go there for French-language immersion courses), their presence somewhere over the southern horizon queerly haunted my thoughts in the city—so resolutely foreign still out there, so utterly separate, a department of France behaving, so close to Mayor Murphy's homely bailiwick, with such absolute damned Frenchness.

The world has been passing through St John's certainly for a longer time, and perhaps with a greater intensity, than through any other Canadian city—from the Basques, Dutch, French, and English of the early years to the GIs of the Second World War and the Russian and Japanese seamen who are familiars of the place today. All their influences have been absorbed, in one degree or another, into the city's persona. To take two oppositely alcoholic examples (for St John's loves its drink): the rum called Newfoundland Screech, born out of the eighteenth-century Caribbean saltfish trade, is bottled in St John's to this day, while Newman's Celebrated Port Wine, originally sent here to mature because the long sea voyage from Europe was said to have a beneficial effect upon it, is offered still under the antiseptic auspices of the Liquor Corporation.

Such range, for a city of 100,000 souls, longitude 52°43' W, latitude 47°34' N! No wonder St John's, though long reduced to the condition of a provincial capital, remains so defiantly itself. There is no false modesty here. 'You're right, but it isn't true of St John's,' a man told me when I remarked that the citizens of most Canadian cities wanted to talk about nothing but themselves—and he went on to rehearse in loving and elaborate detail all other superiorities of the civic character.

In fact the people of St John's are irresistible talkers about themselves, and their peculiar accent, which strikes me as a cross between Irish, Devonian, and Atlantic Seal, makes the flow of their infatuation all the more unguent. Since everyone seems to know nearly everyone else, throughout my stay I felt myself encompassed within a web of overlapping reminiscence, amusement, and complaint. Gossip flows lively in St John's; images of scandal, joke, and mischief passed before me like figures on a wide and gaudy screen. The moneyed dynasties of the town, the Ayres, the Jobs, the Harveys, the Outerbridges, were dissected for me in richest idiom whether living or extinct; politicians suffered the sharp sting of Newfoundland iconoclasm; as I was guided around the streets one by one the pedigrees and peccadillos of their structures stood revealed. Here was the store which was all that was left of the Xs' fortunes, here the mansion where the wildly successful Ys resided. One of the less estimable of the lieutenant-governors lived in this house, a whiz-kid entrepreneur had lately installed eight bathrooms in that, and down by the waterfront was the not very upmarket department store whose ownership had given Mayor Murphy his affectionate nickname.

All this makes life in the city feel remarkably immediate. There is no lag, it seems, between introduction and confidence. By my second day in town I was being given under-the-counter comments on the local judiciary by a well-known politician. By my third day I was being treated to the lowdown about some spectacular financial goings-on. Hardly had I been introduced to a member of one of St John's oldest families, who has one house in town and another on its outskirts, in a kind of Newfoundland version of the transhumance system—hardly had I met this distinguished citizen and his wife than they were explaining why their cat is named after—well, I had better not say who it's named after, let alone why.

I was walking along a city street one day when a man sweeping leaves launched upon me without warning an obviously political statement in such advanced Newfoundlandese that I can only reproduce it impressionistically, so to speak, with the help of a glossary of the dialect. It sounded something like: 'Sish yarkin trapse John Murphy, tacker snarbucklerawny yok John Crosbie, glutch aninst Suzanne Duff.' He looked at me expectantly for a response, so I simultaneously shook my head and nodded, to be on the safe side.

    1 Extend Arm (says a notice at a pedestrian crossing outside City Hall)
    2 Place Foot on Street
    3 Wait Until Cars Stop
    4 Thank Driver

It struck me as a quintessentially St John's announcement, with its blend of the amiable, the unexpected, and the tongue-in-cheek. If reading this essay makes you too feel rather as though you are being slapped in the face with a dried codfish, that is because I was beguiled by almost everything about the city and its inhabitants (almost, because I do wish they wouldn't smoke so much . . .). I dare say that if the long-promised oil bonanza ever happens the town will ruin itself with affluence, but I rather think not: like Aberdeen, it is too rooted in the satisfaction of being utterly unlike anywhere else.

The standard history of St John's is a monumental two-volume work by Paul O'Neill. One might expect such a labour of municipal devotion to be heavy going; in fact it is one of the most consistently entertaining history books I have ever read, full of excellent stories, gamy characters, and surprising historical allusions. Similarly every corner of old St John's offers its own intriguing details. At 100 Water Street there is the sweetly old-school china shop that the Steele family has run for more than a century, while not far away the Neyle-Soper Hardware Store displays in its windows, like *objets d'art* in the museum, grandly Newfoundland things like paraffin lamps, hatchets, scythes, and mousetraps that catch four mice at a time. There is a shop that sells nothing costing more than three dollars, and a shop that sells Young Seal Carcass at 49 cents a pound, and Kim Le's Tailor Shop with tailoring visibly taking place inside. Above the old lovers' steps of McMurdo's Lane the starlings roost in their noisy thousands.

See that object on the rooftop there? That's the periscope of a German U-boat, mounted triumphantly above the Crow's Nest club, which was a famous haven of the convoy captains in the Second World War. See those wagons beyond the dockyard? That's the rolling stock of the narrow-gauge Newfoundland Railway, forlornly immobilized here because the railroad no longer exists. Hear that bang? That's the gun on Signal Hill, fired each day at noon as it has been since the days of the redcoats.

As for the concrete City Hall, it is a very repository of the civic self-esteem. Such banners and plaques and portraits and statues and old municipal photographs! Such ship models and armorial bearings and fraternal messages from admirals, mayors, and societies of merchant venturers! When I remarked how proper it was that the mayor's own office should look directly down upon the historic waterfront, some-body said yes, and directly down upon his own store, too—such is the organic frankness of this close-hauled sceptic town.

All the same, I was always conscious, as I wandered so enjoyably through the city, that life and history have never been easy here. Beneath the charm there lies a bitterness. St John's is full of disappointment, and is an exposed and isolated place in more senses than one. One afternoon, by driving the few miles out to Cape Spear, I made myself for a moment the easternmost person in North America, and was chilled to think, as I stood there in the wind, that while at my back there was nothing but the ocean, before me there extended, almost as far as the imagination could conceive, the awful immensity of Canadian rock, forest, prairie, and mountain. St John's is the edge of everywhere, the end and start of everything. The sign for Mile 'O' of the Trans-Canada Highway stands immediately outside City Hall; it was on Signal Hill that Marconi received the very first radio communication from across the ocean. Hawker and Grieve failed indeed to fly across the Atlantic from St John's, but Alcock and Brown succeeded, and here one evening in 1927 people hearing the drone of an aircraft ran outside to see Lindbergh's *Spirit of St Louis* disappear into the twilight for Paris.

And to this day, though much of the activity of St John's has moved inland, everything in this city looks down, if only metaphorically, to the Narrows. Even the stolid Confederation Building, erected with a becoming diffidence well back from the bloody-minded seaport, peers cautiously from its distance towards that dramatic fissure. I found myself bewitched by it: repeatedly driving up to its headlands, or around the southern shore to the lighthouse at the end, or waving goodbye to the ships as they trod carefully between the buoys towards the open sea—a distant slow wave of an arm, from wheelhouse or forecastle, returning my farewell as seamen must have responded down all the centuries of Atlantic navigation.

Once I was contemplating that hypnotic view from the bar of the Hotel Newfoundland, which looks immediately out to the Narrows and the Atlantic beyond. It was evening, and the prospect was confused by the reflection, in the plate-glass windows, of the people, plants, and ever-shifting patterns of hotel life behind me. Beyond this insubstantial scene, though, I could see the stern outline of the cliffs, the floodlit Cabot Tower on Signal Hill, the white tossing of the ocean breakers, and the slowly moving masthead light of a ship sliding out to sea.

The hotel pianist was playing Chopin—and as he played, with the recondite inflections of Newfoundland conversation rising and falling around me, mingled with laughter and the clink of glasses, somehow the riding light of that ship, moving planet-like through the mirror images, brought home to me with a frisson the grand poignancy that lies beneath the vivacity of St John's. I thought it sad but exciting, there in the air-conditioned bar.

Refresher Course

*T*his little essay was written for the Independent, *London, at the moment when the Americans and their allies were preparing to fall upon Iraq in Operation Desert Storm. I found myself greatly depressed by the public attitudes of the United States, as I very often do, but was soon cheered up (if only for the moment) by the private styles of San Francisco.*

THE US immigration official was one of the surly kind. President Bush was getting on my nerves. Operation Desert Shield made my blood run cold. All in all I was hardly in the mood for the Home of the Brave when I flew out of dear old Canada for a day in San Francisco. 'Why do you come here so often?' unpleasantly demanded the immigration man, eyeing my well-stamped passport, and just for a moment I was tempted to answer in kind.

But if there is one place in the United States where private styles make up for public images, it is San Francisco, where all lapsed lovers of America, even loyalists like me experiencing spasms of disillusionment, should be taken for refresher courses. The tides of all-American conformity beat vainly against the San Franciscan rock. I do not sense much of the power or dazzle of America in this resolutely picturesque city; for that you must cross the Bay to Oakland, or look to the ships ever passing beneath the Golden Gate. Instead I find here older aspects of the American genius, like tolerance, and quirk, and gentlemanliness, and kindness, and a touch of the rapscallion lazy.

For my own tastes these are not usually enough. I am generally much more enthralled by Los Angeles, truly one of the great cities of the world. If it's charm I need, after all, I might just as well stay at home in Wales. At those recurring moments of history, though, when the United States flaunts itself at its most interfering and militarist, when the overriding image of the American is a man in a camouflage suit and spookily Nazi-looking helmet, when the fate of the nations is reduced to the status of an American interest—at moments like this the easy-going, entertaining, slightly ineffectual feeling of San Francisco is like a benediction.

Of course it has its flip side. I walked out of my hotel that morning directly into the particular stretch of Market Street, the main drag of downtown San Francisco, which has long been haunted by the city's castaways, layabouts, and beggars. A walk down this sad block or two is certainly a useful corrective to any vision of the USA as a gleaming armoured behemoth. Sick, maimed, half-crazed, stunted, pushing one another about pitifully distorted in wheel-chairs, begging, leaning vacantly against walls or stretched apparently in coma on the pavements, these Americans of many colours look as though they are one and all the victims of some appalling nuclear catastrophe, and they very soon drove any thought of a master race out of my mind.

Mostly, though, San Francisco's reassurances that day were of a genial and essentially bourgeois kind. I spent most of the time just mooching around town, being comforted by the human scale of the place and the sweet temper of its people. Here is a poster on a lamppost offering a reward for Tux the cat, 'who has just moved here from Seattle and is still frightened and disoriented'. Here a lady leaning from her balcony admires the flowers and foliage in the gully below and remarks to me out of the blue, as I come sauntering by, 'Sometimes I thank God just for making that particular tree down there.' Joggers say 'Hi', doormen say 'Beautiful day but we could do with some rain'. In the coffee shop where I pause for elevenses literary-looking persons left over from the beatnik age sprawl artistically over what I take to be unfinished novels, while tieless and stubbled post-yuppies huddle mathematically around laptops. At the restaurant where I have lunch I offer a smile to four twinkling elderly citizens at the next table; they wonder if they know me, discuss the problem audibly among themselves, and decide that, whether they do or not, they will one and all wave merrily back.

It is hard to imagine this people as the citizenry of the greatest military power on earth, with 400,000 men at this moment preparing for war against a faraway country they know decidedly little of. War fever was the last thing in the air of San Francisco. I saw not a single uniform, and the local papers were full of letters denouncing the president's gung-ho postures. Jolly crowds were inspecting the recently restored murals in the Coit Tower, which, with their Marxist progressive imagery, once outraged conservatives and are still enough to make a marine general's medals jangle. Those elderly laughing gentlemen at lunch-time probably fought honourably in World War II, those hirsute novelists were very likely in Vietnam or Korea, but educated young San Franciscans, young and old, seem to me as truly unbelligerent a people, as genially unregimented, as amiably disposed, as any on earth.

Indeed, I found it hard to fancy a single soul I met that day wanting to throw America's weight around the world, willingly dropping a bomb upon an Iraqi, or even being disagreeable at an immigration desk. I was restored to loyalty! That evening I did a signing session at a lovely bookshop called A Clean Well-Lighted Place, sustained by cappuccino brought in from the Italian café next door. A marvellous variety of San Franciscans came to have their books signed. There were eminent professional persons who made me feel flippant. There were radiant aspirant authors who made me feel aunt-like. There were cheerfully self-declared sufferers of AIDS. There were astonishingly wrinkled and cosmeticized old ladies. There was a man planning to write a biography of Beverley Nichols. There was a man I had met at an airport twelve years before, and three elegant and articulate dames turned out to be transsexuals.

Half-way through a young man arrived, placed a scribbled family tree before me, and declared himself my cousin George. I had never heard of him in my life before, but how gratified I was to meet him, and to think that I had more than a mere sentimental stake in the city of San Francisco, but was actually, if only three times removed, related to it! SUCKS TO RUDE US IMMIGRATION OFFICERS, I wrote on a wall as I walked back to the hotel that night.

Well, I didn't, actually. But another couple of days in San Francisco, and I might have.

| R | O | U | S | S | I | L | L | O | N |

An Invented Country?

*R*oussillon has a special meaning for me because for some reason or other I sense an arcane link between its presiding mountain, Canigou, and my own favourite mountain at home, Arennig Fawr—a link felt also, though I did not know it until lately, by the artist J. D. Innes, who was similarly bewitched by both. Fortunately there is not too much mystic guff in this essay about the Département, which was originally written for the New York magazine Esquire.

WE stand in the graveyard of the oddest little church imaginable, a cupola on a triangle on a trefoil, among a forest of wrought-iron memorial crosses festooned all over with flowers real and artificial. Across the plain, on a commanding slope, there broods a grave grey fort, huge flag above its gate. In the gulley below an electric train of three canary yellow carriages is labouring its way towards the immensely ribbed and snowy mountains in the distance—which are, as it happens, in another country, under the joint suzerainty of a president and a bishop. We are not very far from Ur, Hix, and Molitg. Llo is just along the road. If we drove a few miles we would see the great mound of Llivia and the Solar Tower.

An imaginary place? Only in the Creator's mind. We are in a mountain churchyard of Roussillon, the extreme south-eastern depart-

137

ment of France, in the lee of the Pyrenees. The fort over there is
Mont Louis, built by the great fortifier Vaubin against the pretensions
of the kings of Spain. The mountains beyond are the mountains of
Andorra, where the president of France and the bishop of Urguel are
titular heads of state. The train is Le Petit Train Jaune de Gerdagne.
The tower is part of the French government's solar power programme.
The weird place-names are Catalan, and the church at our backs is
the parish church of Planes, originally a mosque some say, one of the
little Romanesque masterpieces which, scattered across Roussillon
among unfrequented hills, up valleys without issue, above tumbled
red-tiled hamlets, give to this place a constant sense of thoughtful
contrivance.

Almost everything in Roussillon feels contrived, actually. Although
since 1798 the former province has been prosaically defined as Le
Département des Pyrénées Orientales, still this feels like a small
country of its own, so separate and self-contained is it, so different
from anywhere else, and so curiously complete. It is like a geographical exhibition. About the size of Massachusetts, Roussillon consists
essentially of a roughly circular plain, almost unimaginably fertile,
debouching into the Mediterranean at one end, ringed everywhere
else with highlands, and with a single splendid mountain mass, the
Canigou, protruding emblematically in the middle.

In each of its parts most things are, so to speak, more so. There is
nothing middling here. No mountains are more absolutely mountain-
ous than the grand forbidding ranges of the Pyrenees, all gorges and
sudden snow-bowls, with eagles, bears, and wild goats in them. No
plain could be more allegorically fecund than the irrigated flatlands,
where the peaches and vines are cherished in rolling seas of fertility,
and the sun-flaked villages are awash in early vegetables. The coast of
Roussillon is a didactic mixture of picturesque small ports and appalling
tourist complexes, while the one big city of the country, Perpignan, is
everybody's notion of a Mediterranean town—cavernous cathedral,
fierce citadel, tree-lined boulevards, red wine at pavement cafés,
Arabs, orange trees, and impossibly elegant shop assistants.

It is Perpignan, but it is also Perpinya. Roussillon has been in
France since 1659, when Spain conceded the area, but it is still not
exactly of France. Its people are mostly Catalans, and their homeland
here is only the northern half of the ancient entity whose metropolis
is really Barcelona. The history of Roussillon is inextricably linked

with the history of the Spaniards, and misty Iberian potentates march repeatedly through its annals—monarchs of Aragon and Castile, counts and prelates of Barcelona, Queen Anne of Aragon, King Jaime of Majorca . . .

To the physical display of the place there is thus added a literary kind of quality, for through the daily life of Roussillon the two cultures of this littoral, the French and the Catalan, creatively act upon each other, making for grand themes and theatrical situations. On the one hand the great flag of France flies everywhere, and all the glitter of the French civilization, its books, its films, its worldliness, its imagination, infuse the place with urbanity. On the other there sounds the reedy music of the *sardana*, the Catalan dance of dances, and ever and again you may see a French place-name scratched out in black, and its Catalan version substituted in the vivid red and yellow—sand and sun!—that are the Catalan colours.

Want to meet a Roussillon nationalist? Look there then—could anyone be more utterly nationalistic than Juan there, striding up from the waterfront now, with his great bushy beard, his sandals, his corduroy jacket with a book stuck in its pocket and a Catalan badge in its lapel, and the fierce passion of patriotism that flames from his eyes? The wandering writer has it easy in Roussillon. This country offers its characters freely, as it provides its own plots, and its own strange, haunting, and sometimes bitter *mise-en-scène*.

At two in the morning I decided that enough was enough, and clambering upstairs I knocked upon the door of M. le Propriétaire's private apartment. It sounded as though they were having a football game inside, and sure enough, when the door opened it was the hotel owner's 3-year-old-son, all flushed and tousled with hilarity, who first poked his nose through the crack. 'A million pardons, Madame,' came his father after him. 'How can you forgive us? We were having—how do you say it?—a little practice match!'

I was wide awake by then anyway, and entirely mollified by this explanation I stood on my balcony and looked out across Collioure fitfully sleeping in the light of a half-moon. To the left, beyond the harbour mole, the sea was flecked with white choppy waves; to my right the town stood baked against its vineyard slopes; and all around were the high bare mountains, ridge on ridge against the sky. The little port seemed to be sheltering there, wrapped around in rock against unspecified enemies of sea and hinterland.

Even at its prettiest Roussillon is seldom a gentle place. That generous plain has a harsh and flinty look, much of the coast is cruel black rock and bare headland, and the up-country hills are often disturbingly tinged with green metallic bands and layers of rusty ochre. The silhouettes of Roussillon tend to be spiky. The wines are never bland, whether they be the tangy white wines of the interior, or the peculiar red of Banyuls on the coast, which looks a bit like syrup of figs and tastes like a thousand-year-old Madeira. The food is pungent, sometimes brutal—shellfish, wild duck, mighty paellas, sea-stews, mushrooms, culminating for my own tastes in the great Catalan confrontation called *mel i mato*—sour cream cheese covered with honey.

The people too are bittersweet people, people of sly smiles and dry humours. They observe you cannily out of the corners of their eyes even as you are observing them over your notebook in the café, and are to be observed in the mirror above the bar discussing you in slightly amused undertones as you leave. Half-Spanish, half-French, they are a blend of all that we associate with those two peoples, controlled but passionate, exquisitely courteous but down-to-earth, kind but not, I suspect, sentimental—one often senses, in conversation as at the dinner table, that tang of the cheese beneath the honey.

All too often, down the great scoop out of the mountains that is Roussillon, across that plain of fruit and vines, there comes gusting the tireless wind called the *tramontane*, headachy in the summer, raw out of the winter snows. It seems to scour the place of sham or softness, whittling the limestone highlands into spectral forms, sweeping devilish through the twisty gorges of the foothills, and insolently buffeting the high forts and castles that ring this country all around.

There are castles everywhere. From the sinister castle of Salses, like a grounded ironclad at the northern entrance to the plain, to the walls of Prats de Molle deep in the southern mountains, wherever you look you may discover a fortress, sometimes crumbled and deserted, sometimes still waking you with a blast of bugles at breakfast time. Even as I looked out across Collioure that night of the football game, there came stealing out of the dark sea a flotilla of inflatable canoes, paddled by silent soldiers in camouflage suits, back after exercises to their quarters in the former summer castle of the king of Majorca.

All this is partly the frontier condition. Roussillon has always been frontier country. It has smuggled fugitives, resisted invasions, disputed border-lines all down the centuries, and one is conscious always of customs posts and striped barricades never far away. There are the high wild crossing-stations, far up among the snows and the ski-lifts, which mark the beginning of Andorra. There is the huge railway station at Corbières, on the Spanish border, the frontier depot *par excellence*, where you awake as in old movies to the hiss of steam, the clang of couplings and the cry down the corridor of 'Passeports, Mesdames, messieurs, passeports, s'il vous plaît . . .'

For centuries the tides of power swept repeatedly across this corner of Europe. Hannibal marched this way, the Moors came, the feudal powers of the Middle Ages battled for their petty supremacies and the new nation-States clawed their way into existence, Aragon and Catalonia, Provence and Toulouse welding themselves into France and Spain. Of all these conflicts, now mostly confused in the memories of the peoples, the saddest were the campaigns by which the forces of religious orthodoxy, in the thirteenth century, exterminated the society of the Cathars, those revolutionary heretics whose ideas were to give birth in the end to all the horrors of the Inquisition.

The Cathars, besieged on all sides, put up their last doomed resistance in the rocky hills of northern Roussillon, and there their final refuges remain—castles inaccessible as eyries on those windy heights. They are known to the publicists as Les Citadelles du Vertige, and look from the valleys below to be very embodiments of defiant zealotry, but when you get closer they come to seem more forlorn than fanatic. An iron chain helps you up the final slippery slope to the highest, loneliest and last of them all, Queribus, and clambering up there in the howling wind, to the cold wreck of a fortress that stands at the top, gives you a sensation not of heroism, but of unutterable abandonment.

'Ah,' said a man to whom I voiced this thought, 'but up there the Cathars were close to their God. Why else were they at Queribus?' It is true that their faith was ascetic, self-punishing, and true too that Roussillon as a whole has to its character something essentially austere and unworldly.

It is a holy country, where hermits and meditatives have always pursued their silent métiers. Sometimes Christianity in Roussillon is honoured in the flamboyant Mediterranean way, with hooded penitents processing with images in Holy Week, and macabre effigies of martyrdom. More often it seems a stark and lofty faith. Stern in the flanks of mountains crouch the great Romanesque monasteries: Saint-Martin-du-Canigou silent but for the squawking of jays and the tapping of woodpeckers on its wooded belvedere, or Saint-Michel-de-Cuxa, whose Catalan monks breed German shepherd dogs, and whose medieval cloisters were to become the nucleus of the Cloisters Museum in New York. Defiantly everywhere stand the little Romanesque churches, like that shamrock-shrine of Planes, with their rough-tiled roofs, the figures of cats, saints or death's heads that ornament their noble porches, and the sturdy belfries that one can see, undaunted by the colossal landscapes all around, minute but majestic in every prospect of Roussillon.

Often such sacred buildings stand all alone, and look as though nobody goes near them from one year to the next, but then a muscular self-sufficiency is part of their power. They are tough, monk-like buildings, some of them snow-bound for months at a time, and in the darkness of their naves, the cold of their cloisters, they guard their faith uncompromising.

The supreme geographical fact of Roussillon is the mountain Canigou, 8,400 feet high, snow-capped for much of the year, which dominates the plain. This is a holy mountain if ever there was one. Its attendant plateau, wild and scrub-covered, is ennobled with monasteries and isolated hermitages, and from almost everywhere in Roussillon you can see its great shapely form, aloof but beneficent, solitary but radiant. It is a strange and marvellous hill.

And the strangest thing about it is this: that often it disappears. In the morning, when you look up there from the seacoast or the vineyards, you will see it standing massively assured; but often in the afternoon, by some trick of the Pyrenean light, some refraction of mist or *tramontane*, it has vanished entirely, and a grey-blue haze has obliterated mountain, foothills, hermitages and all.

In this, as a matter of fact, Canigou may stand for Roussillon in general: for to many people, most foreigners perhaps, this whole country remains no more than half-visible at the best of times. Though it has ski centres in the high mountains, raucous new beach resorts, lovely architecture to explore, hot springs to cure rheumatism, strong wines to ease melancholy, a bold cuisine, a terrific jumble of history, unbeatable landscapes and a rich mix of cultures, it has never become one of the world-celebrated holiday destinations of France.

Artists have always loved it (Matisse, Dufy, Derain, and Picasso all worked in Roussillon) but to the great vacationing public it has remained only a name—hardly that indeed, for even travellers of sophisticated experience often have to look it up in an atlas. In their hundreds of thousands the tourists rush down the autoroute from Carcassone on their way to Spain, helter-skelter across the vineyard plain, sweeping past Perpignan without a pause. It takes them perhaps half an hour to cross Roussillon from north to south. To the right they may see Canigou, or they may not; and beyond it the interior of Roussillon is only a transient blue.

All its wonders, all its colours, those sad castles in the wind, the flame of Catalan patriotism, the forts and the little train, the sweet desolation of the mountain oratories—all are out of sight, out of mind. It is almost as though someone has invented them, for an essay perhaps.

| B | E | R | L | I | N |

The Worst Over

This essay, written for Travel Holiday *in New York, recorded a particular moment in the history of Berlin: the moment in 1990 when the infamous Wall was opened, and for the first time in nearly half a century one could travel freely from one part of the city to the other. The Wall still stood, when I wrote it, two separate governments ruled Germany, and there was still a colossal difference between East and West Berlin: but I was describing the very last days of a historical phenomenon.*

I SAT over my victuals in the Kurfurstendamm, in a Berlin now all but undivided by its wretched Wall, and to the strains of 'Down by the Riverside' from a street musician with a monotonous guitar, I looked into my mind—and my heart, too, since I am of a certain age—to see what images already loitered there of this infamously ambivalent city.

I found emblems of iconoclastic fun and freedom, and comfortable hausfrau emblems of flower boxes and sticky cakes, and Le Carré suggestions of the sinister mingled with the seedy, and above all, perhaps, symbols of terrifying power wrestling with tragedy. But I have been visiting this city intermittently since soon after the Second World War, and realizing that afternoon that my own perceptions of Berlin had been blurred by time and myth and old emotion, I reluctantly tipped the lugubrious troubadour and set out to wander the city districts, east and west of the crumbled ideological border, to discover which of my mental images were still recognizable on the ground.

I did not have to look far for the fun. The top end of the Kurfurstendamm, the showiest boulevard of West Berlin, offers perhaps the liveliest and least inhibited street scenes in all Europe. Beneath the glare of the neon signs, past the crowded pavement cafés, flooding through the tumultuous traffic in cheerful jay-walk, an endlessly vivacious young populace laughs, struts, sits around, eats, plays music, kisses, and shows off from the break of afternoon until the end of dawn.

It is like a perpetual fair, or perhaps a bazaar, the genteel with the rapscallion, the well-heeled with the indigent: gypsy beggars with babies, bourgeois ladies with dogs on leads, lovers embracing at restaurant tables, unshaven money-changers in dark doorways—an elegant wind trio playing Scarlatti outside a brightly lit shoe shop, a not-very-skilful acrobat treading a rope between two trees, tireless drummers, tedious mimes, unpredictable skateboarders, portrait sketchers, hangdog youths with ghetto-blasters squatting among their own rubbish—smells of coffee and fresh rolls, too, double-decker buses sliding by, fountains splashing, pavement showcases of leathers and jewels—and presiding over it all, incongruously preserved there as a reminder of old horrors, the ugly tombed hulk of the Kaiser Wilhelm Memorial church, defiantly floodlit.

Berliners have always been famous for their irrepressible disrespect and hedonism, maintained through all oppressions and apparent even when I first came here to find a city half in ruins. Even on the east side, where the equivalent of Kurfurstendamm is the loveless Stalinist Alexanderplatz, even there, now that the dictatorship has gone, flashes of high spirit show through the authoritarian grumps (fostered not only by forty years of Communism, but by a decade of National Socialism before that). A waiter winks and bypasses the management ruling that we are too late for a cup of coffee. A young man dashingly U-turns his car, with a glorious screeching of brakes and skidding of tyres, across Karl-Marx Allee to pick up his laughing girl. A stretch of the hitherto sacrosanct Wall—the wrong side of the Wall—has been covered with murals and called the East Side Gallery.

Liberty is in the very air of Berlin now. It is good to be alive here, and to be young must be heaven. Everything is in flux, everything is changing, new horizons open and nothing demands unqualified respect of allegiance. Though half of Berlin is the theoretical head-quarters of an about-to-be-disbanded and thoroughly discredited state, the city is not really the headquarters of anything much, and this gives it a stimulating sense of irresponsibility. Tokens of fun abound indeed, and none are more endearing than the preposterous little cars, like goblin cars, that swarm out of East Berlin for a night out or some window-shopping in the West, with hilarious clankings and wheezings of their primitive engines, and faces smiling from every window. It is not the black, cynical fun of *Cabaret*, Dietrich, or Brecht; it seems to me essentially the fun—dare I say it, in Berlin?—of simplicity, even of innocence.

Walking in the woods beside the Muggelsee, in a corner of East Berlin that would have seemed inexpressibly alarming a year or two ago, I heard through the trees a strain of jovial German music—ho-ho, thump-thump music, with a hearty baritone solo punctuated by jolly choruses. I followed it through the quiet paths, along the reedy edges of the lake (overlooked on its distant eastern shore by the grim black factory chimneys of the former Workers' Paradise), and though by the time I reached its source the tune had changed to the old Tom Jones favourite 'Green, Green Grass of Home', still the scene I found there was an epitome of *Gemütlichkeit*—the snug spirit of domesticity, laced with the sentimental, that was my second Berlin image.

'I'm the Boss' was the first T-shirt slogan I saw, on the ample bosom of a housewife dancing a vigorous disco-jig with her decidedly un-henpecked husband. East Berlin was having a public holiday, and at the hotel beside the lake several thousand citizens, great-grand-mothers to babes in arms, were enjoying a family feast in the sunshine. How perfectly they fulfilled my conceptions! How genially they laughed, sang, danced, drank their beer, and ate their pickled pork knuckles! With what indefatigable smiles the two bands alter-nated, one with the old oom-pah-pah, the other exploring the less raucous fringes of rock! As I watched them there, so hearty, so comradely, I recognized how limitless was the strength of Berlin's camaraderie, sustained over tankards and ice-cream cones through war and piece, dictatorship and revolution, hope and disaster, down the generations.

It knows no borders, recognizes no ideologies (Hitler encouraged it in the name of Strength Through Joy, and even the Communists were obliged to allow family reunions across the Wall), and for myself I find a faintly disturbing quality to it, so absolutely is it able to disregard history. I distrust its latent tendency to prejudice—against immigrant Turks, for instance, who are ubiquitous in West Berlin. I dislike its silly aspects, evident all over the city in jokey statuary, gimmicky fountains, and fairly ponderous humour.

The Berlin coziness is an ethos in itself, for better or for worse, and it is inescapable. Here we see it at a modest wedding in Spandau, where the bride in her long white dress, the groom in his high white stock, the priest and amiable altar boys, the intermittently squabbling choir girls, the solitary bespectacled bridesmaid (pink glasses to match her pink dress), the wildly over-accoutred family guests, the casual passersby, and even we ourselves are all embraced within its bonhomie. Here we observe it at an alfresco restaurant in the Grünewald woods, in the persons of two middle-aged ladies, mother and daughter perhaps, giggling over their asparagus, smiling and nodding encouragingly at us, and balancing their purses carefully on the rims of their glasses to stop the chestnut blossoms from falling into their wine.

And it is realized most explicitly at Lubars, at the northern extremity of West Berlin. Lubars is a genuine farming community, surrounded by meadows and marshland within the limits of the great city. It is crystallized *Gemütlichkeit*. There is a pretty village church in a sweet village green; there are farmyards and stables and a restaurant with lace tablecloths. Sometimes a plump farmer trundles by in a trap drawn by two horses, and if you walk out of the village centre you may find a kind of pixie settlement, all enveloped in green, where people live in little toylike houses, attended by gooseberry bushes and small lawns exquisitely trimmed, like Germans in a fairy-tale.

I looked through a big hole hammered in the Berlin Wall, quite near the site of the old Checkpoint Charlie, and saw into the patch of no man's land beyond. It was littered with rolls of discarded barbed wire, surrounded by ruined buildings, and floored with the dismal mixture of sand, gravel and rubble that has resulted from three decades of herbicide—no greenery was allowed to soften the allegory of the Wall, let alone provide cover for escapers. Three East German soldiers were in there, one tilted back on a kitchen chair with his cap over his eyes, the others kicking an old steel helmet about in the dust. The scene was a very epitome of squalor and wasted time.

For yes, the squalor of the Cold War certainly survives in Berlin. Further along the Wall Potsdamer Platz, once the busiest intersection in Europe, is now a dingy wilderness of gravel and miscellaneous huts, through which the traffic passes as across a patch of desert. Verminous wild rabbits hop around down there, anachronistic hippies with headbands and small children protest against this and that outside grubby tents. Not far away hundreds of Poles run a shambled market of trucks and awnings, selling American cigarettes, crude transistors, some bilious-looking cheese, and dismally assorted bric-à-brac; they were guarded, when I was there, by a huge, mastiffy kind of animal, slavering at the jaws, which was not just the most gruesome dog I have ever set eyes on, but the most horrible creature of any species.

Even now, in the centre of Berlin, you know when you are approaching the line of the Wall, whether from the western or eastern side, by an unmistakable air of dubious dereliction: bombed rubbish-strewn spaces, peeling posters, huddles of men in dark clothes, vestigial street marts with stalls and trailers, apparently abandoned vehicles, faded graffiti like KILL REAGAN or PUNKS UNITE, and in the more touristically accessible parts, souvenir huts selling Soviet army caps or bits of the Wall encased in plastic. Nobody knows what to do with this dismal swathe, sweeping through the heart of the city in such an unlovely way; for the moment it is like the pale strip that is left on the human skin, when a bandage is ripped off.

Seediness enough, then, from the days when spies were swapped across this false frontier and young people were murdered just for trying to cross it. But the sinister part of my image? Gone, it seems to me, all gone. Utterly dispersed is the awful fear that used to hang over the Wall like a black cloud, making every crossing from East to West a chill apprehension. The soldiers of the People's Army kick a redundant helmet about a rubble yard, instead of peering over their gun sights from a watch post, and the Democratic Republic's immigration officials, once so terrifyingly robotlike in their zeal, have turned out, to everyone's surprise, to be human after all. The Television Tower above Alexanderplatz, whose bulbous platform used to look like some sleepless, ominous, all-seeing eye, now merely reminds us that if we care to go that way there is a revolving restaurant at the 680-foot level, and an obliging tourist office at the bottom.

All the resonances of the antagonism have gone, too—a whole genre of legends, politics, art and humour made irrelevant overnight. I had a meeting one day with two German officials, one from each side of the former border, itself an appointment that I would have thought a wild improbability ten years ago. Extracting spontaneous responses from them was rather like unpacking particularly fragile pieces of china, so anxious were they both to appear neither overbearing nor apologetic. But I sensed no animosity between them, and no resentment, though one was dressed in the sportiest Western fashion and gave me a handsomely printed visiting card with translations in English and Japanese, while the other wore an ill-cut dark suit without a tie, and offered me only a piece of pasteboard with his name typed upon it and a crookedly stamped logo on the back.

Where now is the power of Berlin, which once made the world cringe before Prussian salute and Nazi goosestep, swastika and rampant eagle? The divided Berlin of our time has possessed no real power, one half having been a mere puppet of Moscow, the other an all-too-obvious advertisement for capitalism. I had to try hard to recognize any symptoms of arrogance in this city.

I felt a few tremors of it, but only a few, among the relics of the frightful Prussian monarchy, especially in the old royal quarter of the city. There huge triumphal columns still stand on overwhelming façades, supervised by scowling lions, prancing griffins, winged horses, heroes and assorted divinities. The enormous dome of the cathedral swells over Marx-Engels Platz (né Lustgarten); helmeted soldiers stamp outside the Memorial to the Victims of Fascism and Militarism (né the New Guardhouse). The Reichstag, rebuilt but still domeless, stands forlorn beyond Potsdamer Platz, and beside the Spree there loom the portentous classical piles of the institutions that proclaimed, in the last half of the nineteenth century, Berlin's resurgent and assertive culture. A battered Brandenburg Gate still dominates the great avenue of Unter den Linden. Between its trees one can almost see, if one really concentrates, the plumed shakos of cavalry colonels, the fierce moustaches of Junkers, or even the open carriage of the All-Highest himself, the Kaiser, the Emperor of all the Germanies, escorted by uhlans from his war ministry to his schloss.

But only just, and still less remains of Hitler's hubris. There is the brilliantly conceived city-centre airport of Tempelhof, the best thing the Nazis ever built, and there is the unfortunately splendid stadium in which, during the 1936 Olympics, Hitler found himself made a fool of by Jesse Owens (who has a street named after him, just around the corner—more than can be said for the Führer). The rest has mostly gone, and to me it all feels drained of menace. That airport is just a visionary airport, that stadium is just a stadium. I can pass the site of the Gestapo headquarters without a tremor. I can survey without a frisson the bump where Hitler's bunker used to be. Goering's fat spectre does not show itself upon the steps of his air ministry. The evil has been exorcized.

As for the post-war structures of consequence, they have no sense of command at all. The official buildings of the Communist East may be vast and overbearing, but they are essentially sterile, without the sap of true virility. The monumental buildings of the capitalist West feel flimsy, impoverished, or contrived: the roof of the Congress Hall collapsed not long ago, the Philharmonic Hall looks as though it has been banged together out of odds and ends, and Mies van der Rohe's design for the New National Gallery was originally used for the Bacardi Building in Cuba. Few cities on earth, in fact, now feel more dismissive of power for power's sake than Berlin, 1990; all the monuments of Establishment, whether curly-wigged Junker Baroque, Nazi Neo-Classical, steel-and-concrete Stalinist Dogmatic, or Capitalist Junk Pile, look a little ridiculous.

Fun, *Gemütlichkeit*, Malignity, Dominance—some of these emblematic qualities I found alive, some mercifully buried. At the end of my stay I searched for another that might represent not my responses to Berlin's past and present, but my intuitions about its future. I went to the Café Einstein, pre-eminently the writer's café of contemporary Berlin, where you can write novels until closing time over a single cup of coffee—I walked over to the Café Einstein, spread out on a table my 1913 Baedeker's plan of Berlin, and looked for omens in it.

It showed a city of great magnificence, compact and ordered around the ceremonial focus of the Brandenburg Gate, with parklands and residential districts to the west of it, offices of state and finance to the east. Where now almost everything seems random, *ad hoc*, or in transition, Baedeker's 1913 plan shows nothing but rational and permanent arrangement. Modern Berlin has no real centre or balance, devastated as it has been by war and fractured by that vile Wall, but the old Berlin was, in its heavy and self-conscious way, almost a model capital.

It is fashionable just now to imagine the city as an imperial capital again—as the future capital of Europe, in fact, at the place where the western half of the continent meets the east. In some ways it feels like an international metropolis already, frequented as it is now by Westerners of every nationality, and by Turks, Romanians, Poles, Arabs, Africans, and gypsies; road signs direct one to Prague and to Warsaw, and at the Zoo railway station you may meet the tired eyes of travellers, peering out of their sleeper windows, who have come direct from Moscow and are going straight on to Paris.

Physically, no doubt, Berlin can be restored to true unity. Already its wonderful profusion of parks, gardens, forests, and avenues, lovingly planted and replanted through peace and war, give it a certain sense of organic wholeness. When the wasteland of the Wall is filled in with new building, when the Communist pomposities of Karl-Marx Allee and Alexanderplatz have been upstaged by the cheerful detritus of free enterprise, we may see the old municipal logic re-emerging too. The focus of life will return to the old imperial quarter, and the Brandenburg Gate will once more mark the transition between public and private purpose.

But metaphysically, my ancient Baedeker suggests, it will be a different matter. The lost Berlin of its plan was built upon victory— the victory over France, in 1871, which led to the unification of Germany and made this the proudest and most militaristic capital on earth. Everything about it spoke of triumph, Empire, and further victories to come. In today's Berlin the very idea of victory is anomalous, and triumph no longer seems a civic vocation. The world at large may still, at the back of its mind, dread the prospect of German reunification and the revival of German power, but in my judgement at least Berlin is no longer a place to be afraid of. I strongly suspect that half a century from now, when this city has finally recovered its united self, it will turn out to be something much less fateful than Europe's capital. It will be a terrific city, beyond all doubt—a city of marvellous orchestras, famous theatres, of scholarship, of research, of all the pleasurable arts—but not, instinct and Baedeker together tell me, the political and economic apex of a continent. If I had to choose a single abstraction to suggest its future, I thought to myself as I ordered a second coffee after all, it would be something fond and unambitious: relief, perhaps, in this city of interesting times, that the worst is surely over.